The Best of Bournvita Quiz Contest

Derek O'Brien was born in Kolkata. He began his professional career as a journalist for *Sportsworld* magazine but soon shifted to advertising. After working for a number of very successful years as the creative head of Ogilvy, Derek decided to focus all his energy and talent on his passion—quizzing.

Today, Derek O'Brien is Asia's best-known quizmaster and CEO of Derek O'Brien & Associates. He is the host of the longest-running game show on Indian television, the Bournvita Quiz Contest, for which he was voted the Best Anchor of a Game Show at the Indian Television Academy Awards for three years in a row. He hosts the longest-running corporate quiz show on television, the Economic Times Brand Equity Quiz, as well. Always innovating and keeping abreast of the times, Derek is also credited with conducting the first quiz on Twitter in 2010. Alongside, he has written several bestselling reference and quiz books.

In 2011, Derek O'Brien was voted to the Rajya Sabha as a Member of Parliament and is the Chief Whip of the Trinamool Congress in the Rajya Sabha.

Stay in touch with Derek through Twitter, where his handle is @quizderek.

Other books by Derek O'Brien

Bournvita Quiz Contest Quiz Book 2012
Ultimate BQC Book of Knowledge (Volumes 1 and 2)
Derek's Challenge
Speak Up, Speak Out:
My Favourite Elocution Pieces and How to Deliver Them

THE BEST OF

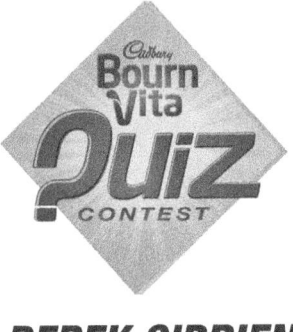

DEREK O'BRIEN

RUPA

Published by
Rupa Publications India Pvt. Ltd 2013
7/16, Ansari Road, Daryaganj
New Delhi 110002

Sales Centres:

Allahabad Bengaluru Chennai
Hyderabad Jaipur Kathmandu
Kolkata Mumbai

Copyright © Derek O'Brien & Associates 2011, 2013

First published in Puffin by Penguin Books India 2011

All rights reserved.
No part of this publication may be reproduced, transmitted, or stored in a
retrieval system, in any form or by any means, electronic,
mechanical, photocopying, recording or otherwise,
without the prior permission of the publisher.

ISBN: 978-81-291-2924-6

Third impression

10 9 8 7 6 5 4 3

The moral right of the author has been asserted.

Contents

Celebrating BQC .... *vii*
Foreword .... *ix*
Hall of Fame .... *xi*
Credits .... *xv*

History-I 1
History-II 7
Language and Literature-I 11
Language and Literature-II 17
Entertainment-I 21
Entertainment-II 27
Geography-I 31
Geography-II 37
Mythology-I 41
Mythology-II 47
Science-I 51
Science-II 57
India-I 61
India-II 67

Wildlife-I	71
Wildlife-II	77
Sports-I	81
Sports-II	88
Mixed Bag-I	92
Mixed Bag-II	98
Answers	102

Celebrating BQC

Let's begin with a quiz question: which is India's longest running television game show? Well, if there were goodies for giving the right answer, thousands of you would have won. Yes! Pucca-pucca, it is the Bournvita Quiz Contest (BQC).

From 1994, millions of television viewers across Asia have made the show into a Sunday morning habit. In an age of quick-fix solutions, breaking news and instant gratification, only some legends endure, and the much-loved Bournvita Quiz Contest is one of them. The programme's iconic status was reaffirmed in 2011 when 'Bring BQC Back', an overwhelming movement on social networking sites, stormed cyberspace. Cadbury India Limited and Derek O'Brien & Associates responded to the call.

The multiple award-winning show is now back. All the goodness of the traditional much-loved format blends with the exciting and the new: the Bournvita Quiz Contest is now bilingual, in English and Hindi. The very able and stunning Saumya Tandon has joined me as co-quizmaster.

The first three new seasons have journeyed through more than 4,500 schools reaching out to lakhs of students across India. Soon, the rest of Asia beckons.

In the years we have lived and breathed the Bournvita Quiz Contest, these words by Rabindranath Tagore written one hundred and fifty years ago inspire and guide us: 'Where the mind is without fear and the head is held high/Where knowledge is free….' We have made this our motto as we strive to 'make knowledge interesting to help young minds grow'.

This book is a special compilation of 1,000 questions and answers from our BQC archives, and is a small tribute to each viewer who flicks the remote on Sunday morning at 10.30 a.m. to watch the brightest minds engage in intellectual combat. We are humbled by your love and hope you will enjoy the book as much as you have loved the show.

Thank you!

With every good wish,
Derek O'Brien

PS: Stay in touch with me through Facebook (www.facebook.com/DOBnA) or Twitter, where my handle is @quizderek.
To know more about me and my company, you can visit my official website at www.derek.in.

Foreword

As the Bournvita Quiz Contest enters its forty-second year, it gives me immense pleasure in introducing to you *The Best of Bournvita Quiz Contest*.

Since its launch in 1948, Cadbury Bournvita has been one of India's most loved and trusted brands. For over six decades, the brand has been an enduring symbol of mental and physical health and all-round development. In 1972, Cadbury India introduced the Bournvita Quiz Contest as a radio programme. Following its tremendous success on radio, the programme found a new avatar on television in 1994. After a hiatus of a few years and following the compelling social media movement to 'Bring BQC Back', 2011 saw the return of India's favourite quiz contest to national television.

This show has touched the lives of over 12 lakh children and millions of loyal viewers through its 600+ television episodes. A number of reputed personalities and celebrities from the fields of cinema, music, sports and politics have also made special appearances on the show.

The Best of Bournvita Quiz Contest is a selection of the very best questions asked on BQC from 1994 to

2010. So if you think you have an unquenchable thirst for knowledge, I am sure you will enjoy this book!

I would like to take this opportunity to thank the team from Derek O'Brien & Associates for producing this book. I would also like to thank the millions of viewers, students, principals and teachers for their love and support, which in turn has made the Bournvita Quiz Contest a household name!

Happy Quizzing!

Anand Kripalu
President, India & South East Asia
Cadbury India Limited

Hall of Fame

PAST WINNERS OF THE BOURNVITA QUIZ CONTEST

1994-1995, Mumbai
Campion High School, Mumbai
Balakrishnan Sivaraman, Sudhanshu Bhuwalka

1995-1996, Mumbai
Kendriya Vidyalaya, Powai, Mumbai
Eipy Koshy, Gourav Shah

1996-1997, Mumbai
Bombay International High School, Mumbai
Nirica Borges, Advait Behara

1997, Mumbai
Mount Saint Mary's School, New Delhi
Joe Christy, Maninder Singh Jessel

1997-1998, Mumbai
Bombay Scottish High School, Mumbai
Shaambhavi Pandyaa, Rahul Lalmalani

1998, Mumbai
Sacred Heart Convent School, Jamshedpur
Ela Verma, Lavanya Raghavan

1998-1999, Mumbai
Indian School Al Ghubra, Muscat
Anand Raghavan, Hitesh Kanvatirtha

1999, Mumbai
Maneckji Cooper High School, Mumbai
Ipsita Bandopadhyay, Gourav Bhattacharya

1999-2000, Mumbai
Chettinad Vidyashram, Chennai
Siddharth, Karthik Das

2000-2001, Mumbai
Bharatiya Vidya Bhavan, Hyderabad
Ananya Bhaskar, Aksha Anand

2001 September, Mumbai
Brightlands, Dehradun
Ankur Bharadwaj, Shray Sharma

2001 December, Mumbai
Little Flower High School, Hyderabad
G. Mithilesh, K Siddharth Reddy

2002 February, Bentota, Sri Lanka
G.D. Birla Centre For Education, Kolkata
Namrata Basu, Rituparna Dey

2002 June, Mumbai
Kerala Samajam Public School, Jamshedpur
Saurav Biswas, Kunal Mohan

2002 September, Mumbai
Jamnabai Narsee School, Mumbai
Sharan Narayanan, Vishnu Shrest

2003 January, Kerala
Naval Public High School, Mumbai
Apoorva Sharma, Abhishek Pandit

2003 May, Kolkata
St. Patrick's Higher Secondary School, Asansol
Pushpen Dasgupta, Shamik Ray

2003 October, Sangla
St. Agnes Loreto Day School, Lucknow
Aastha Srivastava, Illa Gupta

2004 February, Swabhumi, Kolkata
Apeejay School, Jalandhar
Mohit Thukral, Sahil Sareen

2004 May, Goa
Springdales School, Delhi
Anirudh Sridhar, B. Anuraag

2004 July, Indian Military Academy, Dehradun
The Mother's International School, Delhi
Krittika Adhikary, Milind Ganjoo

2004 November, Kolkata
Amity International, New Delhi
Aishwarya Singhal, Adarsh Modi

2005 February, Kolkata
St. Kabir, Ahmedabad
Yogarshi Vyas, Helish Sharma

2005 May, Kolkata
Brightlands, Dehradun
Akshay Sharma, Avantika Singh

2005 August, Kolkata
Amity International, New Delhi
Utkarsh Johari, Aishwarya Singhal

2006 July, Kolkata
Riverdale High School, Dehradun
Kartikeya Panwar, Sumit Nair

2006 November, Kolkata
Seth Jaipuria School, Lucknow
Ratnaksha Lele, Ananya Kumar Singh

2011 August, Kolkata
Amity International School, Noida
Kripi Badonia, Shinjini Biswas

2012 January, Kolkata
Birla Vidya Niketan, New Delhi
Anusha Malhotra, Nitya Bansal

Credits

DIRECTOR	Derek O'brien
CO-QUIZMASTER	Saumya Tandon
EXECUTIVE PRODUCERS	Nayan Chaudhury
	Sunil Shah
	Andrew Scolt
PRODUCER	Prabuddha Chatterjee (Gulu)
ONLINE DIRECTOR	Dongrej Gor
CREATIVE DIRECTOR	Shrradha Kulkarni
DOP	R Diwakaran
SOUND	Ashwyn Balsaver
	Seby Fernandes
SENIOR RESEARCH ASSOCIATES	Amit Ghosh
	Shalini Chaudhury
	Anik Ghosal
	Srirupa Roy
RESEARCH ASSOCIATES	Ammar Hamid
	Ayashman Dey
	Nilanjana Basu

SENIOR RELATIONSHIP ASSOCIATES	Heena Ade (Israni) Fatema Marfatia Sheldon Alliew Aubrey Whyte Dipankar Rao Calvin Tully Laressa Gomez
RELATIONSHIP ASSOCIATES	Durjoy Guha Sean Augustine Conrad Pote Daniel Johns Fionna Sayers Tapan Roy Natasha Gasper
SENIOR DESIGN ASSOCIATE	Mahua Basu
SENIOR FINANCE ASSOCIATE	Kalyanmoy Hazra
SENIOR PRODUCTION ASSOCIATE	Sreevalsa Menon Shane Baptiste
PRODUCTION ASSOCIATES	Vinu Joseph Supriyo Nandi Victor Bhat Michael Blacquiere
SAUMYA'S WARDROBE	Kiran Uttam Ghosh
SAUMYA'S HAIR AND MAKE-UP ARTIST	Elton Fernandez / Shradha Alkunte

OPERATIVE CAMERAMAN	B.lokabiraman
	Bhagyawan
	Anandan
	D.nandakumar
	Debabrata Paul
	Sridhar
HINDI SCRIPT	Rajneesh Kaushal
OFFLINE EDITORS	Vivek Iyer
	Bhavin Patel
JIMMY JIB	Arshad Shaikh
	Saleem Syed
MUSIC	Shankar, Ehsaan, Loy
ASST TO DOP	Selvaraj Xavier
	Selvam.j
SET DESIGN & FABRICATION	Kosmos India
HD EQUIPMENT	Kaliedoxcope
POST PRODUCTION	
SOUND, LIGHTS & AV	Friends Of Shiva
SHOW PACKAGING	
SHOT AT	Aurora Studio
PRODUCTION ASSISTANTS	Pabitra
	Mrinal
	Saha
	Jha
	Sudip
MAKE UP	Babu

HISTORY-I

1. What travelled from the hands of Nadir Shah to Ahmed Shah Abdali to Ranjit Singh and eventually to Queen Victoria and the British royal family?
2. Who did Karl Doenitz succeed as the leader of the Third Reich?
3. 'The saint has left our shores. I sincerely hope forever', wrote a statesman named Smuts. Who was the saint?
4. In 1926, which Indian politician represented the University of Calcutta at the Congress of the Universities of the British Empire?
5. If the Paleolithic Age is also called Old Stone Age, then what is the Neolithic Age called?
6. On 9 August 1974, what did Richard Nixon do that no other US President before him had done?
7. During World War II, what was the code name given to the secret project to develop the atom bomb in USA?
8. According to legend, which instrument did Nero play while Rome burnt?
9. Which famous ruler used a sword named Bhawani?
10. During World War II, who were called the Kamikaze pilots?

11. Which fort's name is derived from a Telugu word meaning 'Shepherd's Hill'?
12. Which Indian leader did Sir S. Ramgoolam pay a special tribute to when he chose 12 March as the Independence Day of Mauritius?
13. Who introduced the practice of *Sijda* (prostration) and *Paibos* (kissing the monarch's feet) in the court as normal forms of salutation to the king in India?
14. After the First War of Independence, to which country was the last Mughal emperor Bahadur Shah Zafar exiled to after the First War of Independence?
15. Who was called 'The Black Pimpernel' during his clashes with the South African authorities?
16. Who was the first woman Prime Minister in the world?
17. Whose life did Nazm, a water bearer, save to be crowned king for half a day at Agra Fort?
18. The hymns of the Rig Veda are divided into ten books. What are they called?
19. Which landmark in Delhi is also known as 'Masjid-i-Jahanuma' or 'mosque commanding a view of the world'?
20. The Marathon commemorates the heroic run of a Greek soldier. Between which two places did he run?
21. Which king wrote *Amuktamalyada*?
22. How did Vladimir Ulyanov get the name Lenin?
23. In the nineteenth century, a group of people known as the abolitionists existed in US What were they trying to abolish?
24. Who lived in China for seventeen years and published his travel anecdotes under the name *Il Milione* (The Million)?

25. In 1922, a police station was burnt at a village near Gorakhpur in Uttar Pradesh forcing Gandhiji to suspend the Civil Disobedience Movement. Name the incident.
26. Which Indian ruler was the historian Lane-Poole referring to when he said, 'He tumbled through life and tumbled out of it'?
27. What lies broken at the feet of the Statue of Liberty?
28. According to the Treaty of Amritsar, which river formed the eastern boundary of Ranjit Singh's territories?
29. Why was Narayan Dattatreya Apte hanged and with whom?
30. Which queen's memorial stands at Phoolbagh, Gwalior?
31. How is Prince Jauna better known in Indian history?
32. Which ruler's original name was Temujin?
33. Whose son was the last Mughal emperor of India?
34. Her parents were William and Fanny. She spent her childhood in a house called Lea Hurst in Derbyshire, England. Her parents named her after an Italian city. Name this well-known person.
35. When Timur invaded India at the close of the fourteenth century, which dynasty formed the Sultanate of Delhi?
36. Which six-letter name links a South African statesman and the Battle of Trafalgar?
37. Franklin D. Roosevelt, a Democratic Party candidate, was elected four times to the post of US President (he was President from 1933 to 1945). Who was the next Democrat to be elected twice to the post?

38. During World War II, if *Il Duce* was Benito Mussolini, who was Der Fuhrer?
39. For which commodity did Mahatma Gandhi undertake a famous march in 1930?
40. Which capital city was formely called Christiana?
41. Which famous leader's body was hung, head downward, in the Piazza Loreto in Milan in April 1945?
42. In which present-day country was the Buddha born?
43. Which king's court was the poet Jayadeva attached to?
44. Which Mughal emperor was Arjumand Bano Begum married to?
45. In which country did Napoleon meet his waterloo?
46. Which war was described as 'the wrong war, at the wrong place, at the wrong time, and with the wrong enemy'?
47. Who was *Time* magazine's 'Man of the Half Century' in 1950?
48. Whose sacred tooth is said to be at Sri Lanka's Temple of the Tooth?
49. Which Indian king did the historian Bana write about?
50. Who gave the name Nivedita to Margaret Elizabeth Noble?

Derek's Fun Facts

HISTORY

1. The Hundred Years' War, the longest war in recorded history, actually continued for 116 years from 1337 to 1453. The war, fought between England and France for the right to the French crown, ran through the reigns of several English and French kings.
2. On 12 March 1930, Mahatma Gandhi started the historic Dandi March to break the Salt Law and on 13 April 1930, C. Rajagopalachari started a march from Tiruchi to Vedaranyam for a similar purpose.
3. According to legend, Shah Jahan, when imprisoned by his son Aurangzeb, spent eight years looking at the Taj Mahal lying on a bed, through a diamond fixed at a particular angle in the wall facing him.
4. The first rockets were built in India by Tipu Sultan some of which were seized by the British army and are currently on display at London's Royal Artillery Museum. An area within Srirangapatna Fort with high walls on three sides measuring nearly 40 feet is reckoned to be Tipu's 'rocket court' or the launch pad.
5. The wars fought in England between the House of Lancaster and the House of York between 1455 to 1485, were known as the Wars of the Roses because the House of Lancaster had a red rose as

its symbol while the House of York had a white rose as its emblem.

6. Hitler dreamed of becoming an artist. He applied twice to the Vienna Academy of Fine Arts in 1907 and 1908 but was denied entrance both times. Hitler left school at sixteen with no qualifications and struggled to make a living as a painter in Vienna.

7. The atomic bomb that was detonated over Nagasaki, Japan, by the United States on 9 August 1945 was code named 'Fat Man'.

8. Timur was white-haired from childhood. He was also lame because as a youth he was struck by an arrow in his right leg, which damaged the leg permanently. Thus, he was called Timur the Lame, which later on became Tamerlane. However he could still ride a horse at full gallop and was a ferocious soldier.

9. The credit for setting up the first professional fire brigade is often given to Napoleon Bonaparte. As the French emperor, he ordered that a division of the French army known as Sapeurs-Pompiers protect Paris with thirty manual fire pumps. However, there were people who were paid to provide some form of fire protection or suppression service in Paris, many years prior to that.

10. It is said that Alexander the Great, Julius Caesar, Genghis Khan, Napoleon, Mussolini and Hitler all suffered from ailurophobia, i.e., the fear of cats

HISTORY-II

1. Which Indian was nominated for the Nobel Peace Prize in 1937, 1938, 1939, 1947 and 1948 but was never awarded the prize?
2. Around the 16th and the 18th centuries, this city was the site of three major battles fought on 21 April, 5 November and 14 January. Name it.
3. Who was the first non-Indian president of the Indian National Congress?
4. Which UNESCO World Heritage site was built on the land of the Kachhwahas of Ajmer?
5. Marie Antoinette persuaded Louis XVI of France to pass a law stating that 'it' had to be square in shape. What was 'it'?
6. Which infamous prison was stormed on 14 July 1789?
7. Which Indian ruler would you associate with a carved wooden semi-automatic tiger mauling a man, first displayed in the East India Company museum in 1808?
8. Which Mughal emperor wrote poetry under the pen name 'Zafar'?
9. In the mid-sixteenth century, for whom did Haji Begum build a tomb?

10. Which dynasty of the 9th century did Vatsaraja, Nagabhatta II and Mihirbhoja belong to?
11. Which was the highest court of appeal in British India for civil matters?
12. Which kingdom was founded by Hasan Gangu in 1347?
13. On 13 May 1940, who told his cabinet, 'I have nothing to offer but blood, toil, tears and sweat.'?
14. Which War ended at 11 a.m. on the eleventh day of the eleventh month in 1918?
15. Which famous Italian artist was born on 6 March 1475 in the village of Caprese, Italy? (Hint: He attracted the attention of Lorenzo de Medici.)
16. Which date is written on the book held by the Statue of Liberty?
17. On which famous ship did Nelson die after being victorious at the Battle of Trafalgar?
18. Which famous Gupta king was the son of the Licchavi princess Kumaradevi?
19. Which ruler ruled with his elder brother untill 445 AD and later murdered him?
20. Which leader served as the first Indian municipal commissioner of Ahmedabad from 1917 to 1924?
21. Which Indian ruler was the first to attack Chittor in 1303 after hearing about Rani Padmini's beauty?
22. What was built for resting troops on land retained after the Anglo-Gurkha War of 1814-1816?
23. Which US President adopted White House as the official name of the Executive Mansion?
24. Which famous Indian freedom fighter was the adopted son of Peshwa Baji Rao II?

25. Which freedom fighter published a pamphlet titled The Green Pamphlet listing the problems faced by Asians in South Africa?
26. Which Mughal queen's name translates into 'Beloved Ornament of the Palace'?
27. Who was known as Sandrakottas to the Greeks?
28. Which gemstone was valued by Babur as 'two-and-a-half days food for the entire world'?
29. Who invited Atomba Singh to teach Manipuri dancing in Bengal in the 1920s?
30. In 1815, which ousted ruler staged a comeback with what is referred to as 'The Hundred Days'?
31. What, according to Gandhiji, was 'the sun of the village solar system'?
32. Which famous leader was Gopalkrishna Gandhi's maternal grandfather?
33. Which leader said: 'Every blow aimed at me is a nail in the coffin of British imperialism.'?
34. In ancient Greece, what was the punishment for cutting down an olive tree?
35. Which World Heritage Site was the island capital of the Konkan Mauryas?
36. The foundation of which landmark in India was laid by Mian Mir Ji in 1588?
37. Which monument in Delhi was designed by Fariborz Sahba?
38. Which metal was first used by humans in the Chalcolithic period?
39. In which present-day state is the historical site of Haldighati located?
40. In 1953, who received the Nobel Prize for Literature

'for his mastery of historical and biographical description as well as for brilliant oratory in defending exalted human values'?

41. Who was the Prime Minister of UK when India became independent?
42. Which famous author of *The Golden Threshold* was so shocked by the Jallianwala massacre that he/she stopped writing poetry after the incident?
43. Which dictator once earned money by selling his paintings after he was refused admission to the Academy of Fine Arts?
44. Which monument was being constructed when 20,000 workmen were accommodated in a small town named Mumtazabad in the 1630s?
45. Which Mauryan king was referred to as 'Amitraghata' in some texts?
46. By what name is Takht-i-Taus better known to us?
47. Which famous Indian freedom fighter was born on 23 January at Cuttack in Orissa?
48. Which country's national anthem was written by Ananda Samarakone?
49. Article 17 of the Constitution of India was adopted with the slogan 'Mahatma Gandhi Ki Jai'. What does it deal with?
50. According to Acharya Vinobha Bhave 'Spirituality + _____ = Sarvodaya'?

LANGUAGE AND LITERATURE-I

1. Which author is the youngest winner of the Nobel Prize for Literature to date?
2. Which book, published in 1852, was smuggled into Russia in Yiddish to evade Czarist censors?
3. On which ancient book is the collection of stories titled *Hitopodesha* based?
4. According to Sikh tradition, which writing system was invented by Guru Angad so that sacred literature could be accurately recorded?
5. For which work did R.K. Narayan win the Sahitya Akademi Award in 1960?
6. Which novel did Charles Dickens write in protest against the Poor Law of 1834?
7. If Antonio was the 'Merchant of Venice', who was the 'Moor of Venice'?
8. According to the idiom, whom do you pay when you rob Peter?
9. Which book describes the essence of animalism as 'four legs good, two legs bad'?
10. Which children's story by Dodie Smith, dealing with dogs, is also a Walt Disney film?
11. Which profession connects Popeye, Captain Haddock

and Sindbad?
12. In the US, this punctuation mark is called a period. What is it called in India?
13. Whose autobiography is titled *An Indian Pilgrim: An Unfinished Autobiography*?
14. Xury was a Moresco boy. Which famous fictional character did he serve?
15. Which author's autobiography is titled *Rasidi Ticket*?
16. Which author said: 'My life in many ways depended on my storytelling abilities, which have been the best and only way in which I have been able to make a living, and also choose the place of my abode, the foothills of the Himalayas'?
17. In nursery rhymes, what is the profession of Little Bo-Peep?
18. Which fictional character, living at the foothills of the Catskill Mountains, slept for about twenty years?
19. Which Shakespearean character said the famous line, 'What a piece of work is man!'?
20. Looked after by Widow Douglas, he escapes, is kidnapped by his father, escapes again and sets down the Mississippi on a raft. Which story is this?
21. Who was the ruler of Alice's Wonderland?
22. What do you call a person who writes books or articles for a more famous person and does not get credit for doing so?
23. On whose novel is Govind Nihalani's film *Hazaar Chaurasi ki Maa* based?
24. In 2003, a newly discovered armoured dinosaur was named in honour of which famous science fiction author?

25. Aeolic and Doric are the two ancient dialects of ...
26. In which book would you come across the great grey lone wolf Akela?
27. What was the pen name of the female author Mary Ann Evans?
28. In which Shakespearean play would you come across the characters Petruchio and Katherina?
29. Which Indian comic-strip character's enemies are Vishkanya and Sonic?
30. Which famous leader's autobiography was translated by Mahadev Desai from Gujarati to English?
31. Which children's author wrote his memoirs *The Fairy Tale of My Life*?
32. Which naturalist is the author of *Tree Tops*?
33. According to the English proverb, what do crocodiles shed?
34. Which book opens with the line 'All children except one, grow up'?
35. Which language was used as the Buddhist canonical language because the Buddha opposed the use of Sanskrit?
36. According to legend, to whom does the sword Excalibur belong?
37. Which character, created by Enid Blyton, lives in Toadstool House?
38. Which popular adventure by R.L. Stevenson was originally titled *The Sea-Cook*?
39. How do we popularly know the author Dhanpat Rai Srivastava?
40. Which novel by Charles Dickens revolves around the character Pip?

41. The adjectives for cat and dog are canine and feline respectively. What is the adjective for horse?
42. 'What immortal hand or eye/ Could frame thy fearful symmetry?' Which famous poem are these lines from?
43. What is the profession of detective Nancy Drew's father?
44. Mrs Hudson is my landlady. My character is based on the surgeon Dr Joseph Bell. I was created by Sir Arthur Conan Doyle. Who am I?
45. Around which religious leader's life do the Jataka tales revolve?
46. Complete the name of this Nobel laureate: Sir Vidyadhar Surajprasad...
47. From which novel is the National Song of India taken?
48. Which kind of an animal is T.S. Eliot's Macavity?
49. Which novel begins with the words: 'Call me Ishmael'?
50. According to the English writer Virginia Woolf, who was 'the greatest of all novelists'?

Derek's Fun Facts

LANGUAGE AND LITERATURE

1. The manuscript of *Swami and Friends* had been making the rounds of London publishers and the last publisher had been requested to send the typescript to R.K. Narayan's friend Purna at Oxford in the event of rejection. He had actually instructed his friend to 'weight the manuscript with a stone and drown it in the Thames'.
2. The author Emily Bronte wrote only one novel in her lifetime: *Wuthering Heights*.
3. A year before Rabindranath Tagore got the Nobel Prize for Literature in 1913, he had lost the manuscript of *Gitanjali* on a trip to England. Tagore, with son Rathindranath and daughter-in-law Pratima Devi, took a train from Dover to London to meet William Rothenstein, a painter. The poet had the manuscript in an attaché case. Arriving in London, they took the underground railway. Awestruck at the 'sight of the modern marvels of the tube', they forgot the attaché case at a station.
4. The Royal Society of Chemistry (RSC) has produced the recipe of Gruel, the notorious dish which Oliver Twist requested more of, after consulting historic sources including Charles Dickens' Victorian novel. It was recreated by French chef Fabian Aid in the RSC kitchen.
5. Stephenie Meyer, author of the *Twilight* series said:

'My female lead was harder. Nothing I named her seemed just right. After spending so much time with her, I loved her like a daughter, and no name was good enough. Finally, inspired by that love, I gave her the name I was saving for my daughter, who had never shown up and was unlikely to put in an appearance at this point: Isabella.'

6. According to William Shakespeare's last will, he left his wife his second best bed.

7. Doris Lessing is now the oldest person to have been awarded the Nobel Prize in Literature. She was eighty-eight years old at the time when she received the honour in 2007.

8. In the Harry Potter series, Hermione's Patronus is an otter because J.K. Rowling likes otters and sees herself in Hermione.

9. Agatha Christie wrote romantic novels such as *Absent in the Spring* (1944), under the pseudonym Mary Westmacott.

10. While a medical student, Arthur Conan Doyle was so impressed by the physician Dr Joseph Bell's skill in observing the most minute details regarding a patient's condition that he modelled his literary creation, Sherlock Holmes, on him.

LANGUAGE AND LITERATURE-II

1. Which book was translated into English by Rabindranath Tagore and published in 1912 with an introduction by W.B. Yeats?
2. In which fictional town are Truth Printing Press and Lawley Street located?
3. In 1865, the first edition of which book by an English mathematician was withdrawn because of bad printing?
4. Which was Premchand's last completed novel?
5. According to UNESCO, who is the most translated woman author in the world?
6. Which term in Latin literally means 'and the rest'?
7. Which fictional transport starts from King's Cross railway station platform number 9¾?
8. Which famous Indian poet used the pseudonym Bhanushsingho?
9. In which country is the town of Hamelin, the place where the legendary tale of the Pied Piper is set?
10. Which novel by Jane Austen was initially titled *First Impressions*?
11. What is the surname of the famous author John Ronald Reuel?

12. In Shakespeare's *Macbeth*, whose ghost did Macbeth see in the banquet scene?
13. Which famous English author was born in 1903 in Motihari in present-day Bihar?
14. Which is the first Sanskrit work to be translated into English by the Asiatic Society?
15. Which fictional characters stay at Bayport with their Aunt Gertrude and their parents Laura and Fenton?
16. In fiction, which carpenter created the character of Pinocchio?
17. Who is the youngest woman writer to win the Man Booker Prize?
18. In the books written by Enid Blyton, what are the following collectively called: Laurence and Margaret Daykin, Frederick Trotteville, Elizabeth and Philip Hilton?
19. Which fictional detective made his last appearance in *Curtain*?
20. Which character in *Alice's Adventures in Wonderland* shares its name with a month?
21. *First Folio*, the first collected edition of whose works, was published posthumously in 1623?
22. Which writer of 6th century BCE is famous for a collection of Greek fables?
23. Which Nobel laureate would you associate with the famous verse collection *Barrack-Room Ballads*?
24. Which novel by Jane Austen is about the sisters Elinor and Marianne?
25. Which Booker Prize-winning novel begins with the character Rahel coming back to her childhood home in Ayemenem?

26. Which fictional character was defeated in a duel with the Knight of the White Moon?
27. Which author's suggestion resulted in Krishnaswami Ayyar Narayanaswami shortening his name to R.K. Narayan?
28. Which story by Rudyard Kipling depicted the adventures of an orphaned son of a sergeant in an Irish regiment?
29. Which word describes a part of the human body as well as a part of a book?
30. Louisa May Alcott wrote *Little Women*. Who wrote *Little Men*?
31. Which comic-strip character's leadership was instrumental in the people of Mongo being finally able to rise up against the rule of Ming?
32. Which famous American author was a licensed pilot on Mississippi steamboats?
33. Which novel by Vikram Seth revolves around Mrs Rupa Mehra's efforts to arrange her daughter Lata's marriage?
34. How do we better know the pair Mr Montague and Miss Capulet?
35. In which story by Victor Hugo does Jean Valjean steal a loaf of bread and is imprisoned?
36. Which famous author wrote *Euclid and His Modern Rivals*, a rare example of a humorous work concerning mathematics?
37. 'All for one and one for all' was the motto which famous fictional trio's?
38. Which thirteen-year-old girl wrote about her life in an 'annexe', a hiding place in a building in Amsterdam?

39. 'Never tickle a sleeping dragon' is the motto of which fictional school?
40. Which book by Michael Crichton about prehistoric animals was the basis of a very popular film in 1993?
41. How do we know the 'Pope of Fools' better?
42. Which famous novel by Harriet Beecher Stowe opens: 'Late in the afternoon of a chilly day in February, two gentlemen were sitting alone over their wine…in Kentucky.'?
43. Which Booker Prize winner is the author of *Haroun and the Sea of Stories*?
44. In *The Jungle Book*, what kind of an animal was Tabaqui?
45. Which Indian wrote the volume of poetry called *The Golden Threshold*?
46. Lockwood and Nelly (Ellen) Dean are the two narrators of which classic novel?
47. 'Yours is the Earth and everything that's in it/ And—which is more—you'll be a Man, my son!' Which poem's last lines are these?
48. In Shakespeare's *The Merchant of Venice*, from whose body did Shylock want a pound of flesh?
49. Name a Hindi word entered in the English dictionary meaning 'booty from a robbery'.
50. 'My mother only said/ Thank God the … picked on me/ And spared my children.' In which poem by Nissim Ezekiel would you come across this line?

ENTERTAINMENT-I

1. In 1975-76, which famous film won its only Filmfare Award in the Best Editing category?
2. Who was the first recipient of the Dadasaheb Phalke Award?
3. Which comic-strip character's fifth ancestor crossed swords with the pirate Blackbeard in 1600?
4. Which famous actor played the role of Pawan Raghujan in Mani Kaul's *Idiot*?
5. Who composed music for the Satyajit Ray-directed film *Goopy Gyne Bagha Byne*?
6. Who played Sanjay Dutt's father in the film *Munna Bhai M.B.B.S.*?
7. Which famous singer produced the 1988 film *Lekin*?
8. Who was the first actor to appear on the cover of *Time* magazine?
9. Who took on nine roles in the 1974 film *Naya Din Nayi Raat*?
10. In Tintin comics, what do we compare to tell the difference between Thomson and Thompson?
11. In the famous song from the film *Shree 420*, which accesssory does Raj Kapoor describe as 'Roosi'?
12. Which classical musician composed film music using the name A.R. Qureshi?

13. Who knocked out Amitabh Bachchan and seriously injured him on the sets of *Coolie*?
14. Which Indian comic-strip character's relatives are Bhim and Maya?
15. Which famous actor made his acting debut in the 1969 film *Saat Hindustani*?
16. Which is India's first 3D feature film?
17. The English version of which film directed by Sooraj Barjatya is *When Love Calls*?
18. In Chacha Chaudhary comics series, who is a 'friendly alien'?
19. Which well-known superstar made his debut in a lead role opposite Mamata Shankar in Mrinal Sen's *Mrigaya*?
20. Which well-known entertainer's autobiography is titled *Moonwalk*?
21. Which Indian film-maker was awarded a lifetime achievement Oscar in 1992?
22. Ringo Starr, John Lennon and George Harrison were all members of the group Beatles. Who was the fourth member?
23. In which Hindi film did Amitabh Bachchan do his own playback singing for the first time?
24. Bhanu Athaiya won an Oscar for the costume designing of which much-acclaimed film. Name the film?
25. Who is the latest in the list: Sean Connery, Roger Moore, Timothy Dalton and Pierce Brosnan?
26. Find the connection between the film *Parineeta* and the TV serial *Hum Paanch*.
27. Which comic-strip character's butler is called Cadbury?

28. Which Aishwarya Rai film showed all the Seven Wonders of the World in one song?
29. Who was the story writer of the 1958 film *Madhumati*?
30. What is the connection between Mewati, Agra, Kirana, Gwalior and Jaipur?
31. What would you be watching if you saw Mr Sulu, Scotty the engineer, Dr McCoy and Captain James Kirk?
32. In the film *The Lion King*, Simba was the lion king. What kind of an animal was Timon?
33. Besides creating the comic-strip character Phantom, which other famous comic strip did Lee Falk create?
34. At the National Film Awards, for which category is the Nargis Dutt Award given?
35. Which comic-strip character has an enemy named Kilvish?
36. Which Rajya Sabha MP acted in her first film *Mahanagar* under the direction of Satyajit Ray?
37. Which actress won her first National Award for the film *Ankur*?
38. In comics, if Clark Kent is Superman and Peter Parker is Spiderman, who is Prince Adam?
39. Name the American President who, along with his wife, acted in the film *Hellcats of the Navy*.
40. Who played the role of Richie Rich in the 1994 film *Richie Rich*?
41. In the film *Sholay*, what was the name of Hema Malini's horse?
42. Which famous author played the role of Iqbal Ahmed Khan in *Mr and Mrs Iyer*?
43. Which 1994 Hindi film was dubbed into Telugu as *Premalayam*?

44. My father received a Padma Bhushan in 1976. My wife received a Padma Shri in 1992 and I received a Padma Shri in 1984. Who am I?
45. Which Hollywood actor's original name is Thomas Cruise Mapother IV?
46. Which alien character does actor Leonard Nimoy portray in the television series *Star Trek*?
47. Which mode of transport could fly when the alien ET rode in its basket?
48. Which Indian cricketer acted in the film *Savli Premachi*?
49. Who was the first actor to win the Filmfare Award for Best Actor?
50. In which 2003 film did Hema Malini pair with Amitabh Bachchan twenty years after their last film together?

Derek's Fun Facts

ENTERTAINMENT

1. *Mother India* was nominated for an Academy Award in the Best Foreign Language Film category but lost by just one vote. The winner that year was Federico Fellini's *The Nights of Cabaria*.
2. Harivanshrai Bachchan wanted to name his first son Inquilab but his poet friend Sumitra Nandan Pant named him Amitabh.
3. Dilip Gupta shot India's first colour film, *Ajit*, in 16 mm and then blew it up to 35 mm. He also received the first Filmfare award for cinematography, for the film *Madhumati*.
4. The Cannes International Film Festival is held annually in May at the Palais des Festivals et des Congres, in the resort town of Cannes, in the south of France. It was created on the initiative of Jean Zay, Minister for Education and Fine Arts, with a purpose to rival the Venice Film Festival. The first edition of the festival was originally set to be held in Cannes in 1939 under the presidency of Louis Lumière, but was cancelled due to the declaration of World War II.
5. MGM art director Cedric Gibbons designed the Oscar statuette of a knight standing on a reel of film gripping a crusader's sword. The statuettes presented at the initial ceremonies were gold-plated solid bronze. Due to a metal shortage during World

War II, the Oscars were made of painted plaster for three years.

6. *Sholay* was released on 15 August 1975, but was about to be removed from cinemas because of low attendance figures. After a few weeks, attendance started rising and word-of-mouth publicity made it Indian cinema's highest grossing film (until *Dilwale Dulhania Le Jayenge*, 1995).

7. Guinness World Records certifies Ramoji Film City as the largest Film Studio Complex in the world.

8. Lata Mangeshkar used to compose songs under the name Anandaghan.

9. W.M. Khan was the first playback singer in Indian cinema. He sang for Alam Ara made by Ardeshir M. Irani, in 1931. For the song recordings, only a harmonium and tabla were used, out of the camera range, and the singer sang into a hidden microphone. The song 'De De Khuda ke Naam Par Pyaare' became extremely popular.

10. In India, *Taal* was the first film to be insured.

ENTERTAINMENT-II

1. Which English film had the following tagline: 'Imagine if you had three wishes, three hopes, three dreams and they all could come true'?
2. Who was the first actress to win the Filmfare Award for Best Actress?
3. On which author's work was the film *The Blue Umbrella* based?
4. Who played Mr India in the film *Mr India*?
5. What was the name of the alien in the film *Koi ... Mil Gaya*?
6. Which Bengali film, directed by Satyajit Ray, was completed because the Chief Minister of West Bengal at that time granted funds for film-making under the road development scheme?
7. India's tallest metal statue of a comic-strip character is a tribute to...
8. What character does Dilip Prabhavalkar play in the film *Lage Raho Munnabhai*?
9. Which Raj Kapoor-directed film was released as *Brodigaya* in Russia?
10. Which author's work is the film *Pinjar* based on?
11. The 2003 animated film, *Finding Nemo*, features

which famous geographical landmark?
12. How do we know A.S. Dileep Kumar better?
13. Which Indian Prime Minister made a brief appearance in the 1977 film *Chala Murari Hero Banne*?
14. In which film has Michelle McNally's story been memorably retold?
15. In Scooby Doo comics, what is Shaggy's surname?
16. Who directed the 2005 film *Iqbal*?
17. Which was the first Indian film to open the Locarno Film Festival?
18. In May 2005, which film played for over 500 weeks at the Maratha Mandir theatre in Mumbai, making it the longest-running initial release in the history of Indian cinema?
19. Who was the first Indian actress to be on the jury of the Cannes Film Festival?
20. In which town does the comic-strip character Archie Andrews live?
21. Which character did Ben Kingsley play in the 1982 film *Gandhi*?
22. *Hum Hain Lajawaab* is the Hindi version of which animated film?
23. Which character's name from the film *Sholay* later became the title of a 1988 film directed by Jagdeep?
24. Which animated film was originally titled *King of the Jungle*?
25. Which is the first animated Disney feature film to be based on historical facts?
26. In comics, which rabbit's catchphrase is 'What's up Doc'?

27. Who played the role of Miss Hawa Hawai in the 1998 film *Chhota Chetan*?
28. In the 1990s, who became the first female actor to win the award in the Filmfare Best Villain Award category?
29. Which comic-strip character has a horse named Hero and a wolf named Devil?
30. Who has won more Oscars than anyone else?
31. In Satyajit Ray's *Shatranj ke Khiladi*, who played Wajid Ali Shah, the Nawab of Awadh?
32. In 1931, which film was hailed as the 'first talkie' in Indian cinema?
33. Which is Amitabh Bachchan's only black and white Hindi film?
34. How do we know actor Jatin Khanna better?
35. In Dennis the Menace, what was Mr Wilson's profession before he retired?
36. In the world of entertainment, how is Enrique Martin Morales better known?
37. Who played the title role in the 2002 film *Makdee*?
38. Palash Sen is the lead vocalist of which band?
39. How do we know Pandit Gangadhar Vidyadhar Mayadhar Omkarnath Shastri better?
40. Which Chetan Anand film won the Grand Prix at the first ever Cannes Film Festival in 1946?
41. Which Indian joined Philip Glass and Mickey Hart to compose the instrumental music (score) for the opening ceremony at the Atlanta Olympics?
42. Who is the famous father of the singer Lucky Ali?
43. Who acted in the lead role in the films *The Mask* and *Liar Liar*?

44. Which is the only film to have ever won every single Oscar it was nominated for?
45. Which famous music director's nickname was Pancham?
46. Who recorded an album with a group and quipped, 'We can make it'?
47. Originally called L'il Folks, which comic strip by Charles Monroe Schulz was sold to United Feature Syndicate?
48. Name the Bollywood star whose pet name is Akki.
49. In the children's film *Anastasia*, who gave the voice for the character Anastasia?
50. Which 1976 film was sponsored by 5,00,000 farmers of Gujarat?

GEOGRAPHY-I

1. Which peak was regarded as the highest peak before Mt. Everest was measured?
2. Apart from Q, U, X and Z, which letter is not used to begin the name of a hurricane in the Atlantic?
3. Lake Kawaguchi is noted for reflecting the image of which mountain on its waters?
4. In 1502, which city was named after the Portuguese words for 'river' and 'January'?
5. There are three US states which start and end with the letter 'A'. Name them.
6. Which river, referred to as Namade by Ptolemy, forms the traditional boundary between North India and South India?
7. Nowshak is the highest point of which neighbouring country?
8. Which mountain in Africa has three volcanic centres: Shira, Kibo and Mawenzi?
9. Which lake, apart from Erie, Huron, Ontario and Michigan, is a part of the Great Lakes?
10. In which continent are 'the eight-thousanders', the fourteen mountains on Earth that are higher than 8,000 metres, located?

11. Which Indian state was once known as Lushai Hill District of Assam?
12. Which natural disaster was the cause of mass destruction in the Italian city of Pompeii in AD 79?
13. Which lake holds twenty per cent of the world's total surface fresh water?
14. Which is the largest Asian country with one time zone?
15. Which is the second largest island in the world?
16. Which river is formed by the streams Blue, White and Atbara?
17. Which city was the capital of Odisha before Bhubaneshwar?
18. Which waterfall comprises Horseshoe, American and Bridal Veil?
19. Icelandic, Hawaiian, Strombolian, Vulcanian, Pelean and Plinian are six major types of which geographical feature?
20. If you are writing the names of the union territories of India alphabetically, which name will appear on the top?
21. Which state was carved out of Bihar in 2000?
22. After which leader is Vietnam's largest city named?
23. Which mountain is commonly regarded as the highest summit in the Western Hemisphere?
24. Which Indian state has districts named East Godavari and West Godavari?
25. In Sikkim, the name of which mountain means 'Five Treasuries of the Great Snow'?
26. In his travelogue, which island did Marco Polo refer to as the 'Island of females'?

27. Which sea has been called the 'incubator of Western civilization'?
28. Oman ends with the word 'man'. The name of which country in Asia ends with the word 'men'?
29. Which is the largest landlocked country in the world?
30. On which African river are the Victoria Falls?
31. According to legend, the name 'Andaman' has derived from the word…
32. Which waterbody is called *Khalije Fars* in Persian?
33. Which state is famous for its Kurinji flowers that bloom once in twelve years?
34. Which is the highest continuously active volcano in the world?
35. The name of which capital city means 'eastern capital'?
36. Upon completion in 1931, it was called the All India War Memorial. How do we know it today?
37. Before 1856, which mountain peak was referred to as Peak XV?
38. In 1542, when the Portuguese first sighted the island of Taiwan, what did they name it?
39. Which is the highest peak in the Western Ghats and South India?
40. What is Nek Chand's contribution to Chandigarh?
41. Which is the largest state in India in terms of area?
42. Which Indian town was once divided into Ville Noire and Ville Blanche?
43. Where did the two R's, Roald Amundsen and Robert Peary reach for the first time?
44. Which landmark in Uttar Pradesh was built in 1784 as a food-for-work relief measure during a famine?

45. The ruins of which ancient university lie 62 km from Bodh Gaya and 90 km south of Patna?
46. Which 175-feet-high structure did Akbar build to commemorate his victory in Gujarat?
47. Name the place of worship which stands in the middle of the Amrit Sarovar.
48. Which medieval minaret is also the highest stone tower in India?
49. In India, which famous building, built in 1931, used 700 million bricks and three million cubic feet of stone?
50. Other than India, the name of which Asian country begins with the letters 'Ind' and ends with 'ia'?

Derek's Fun Facts

GEOGRAPHY

1. The names of hurricanes are chosen from a list selected by the World Meteorological Organization. Each name on the list starts with a different letter; for example, the name of the first hurricane of the season starts with A, the next starts with B, and so on.
2. In the mid-19th century, Radhanath Sikdar, a graduate from the Presidency College (then Hindu College) in Kolkata, joined the Great Trigonometric Survey of India. Among many of his accomplishments, the most important was achieved when he compiled data about Peak XV of the Himalayas from six different observations and concluded that it was the tallest in the world. It was later named Mt. Everest after a former head of the Great Trigonometric Survey.
3. The Chinese word for solar eclipse is *shih*, meaning 'to eat'. In ancient China people traditionally beat drums during a solar eclipse to scare off the 'heavenly dog' believed to be eating the sun.
4. The Caspian Sea, Dead Sea, and Aral Sea are actually saltwater lakes.
5. In 1803, a man named Luke Howard used Latin words to categorize clouds. Cirrus, which means 'curl of hair', is used to describe high, wispy clouds that look like locks of hair.

6. According to scientists, the earthquake that generated the great Indian Ocean tsunami of 2004, is estimated to have released the energy of 23,000 Hiroshima-type atomic bombs. On December 26 of that year, the tsunami shook the ground violently unleashing a series of killer waves that sped across the Indian Ocean at the speed of a jet airliner.
7. The famous Gian Lorenzo Bernini project, Four Rivers Fountain in Rome, was completed in 1650 in the Piazza Navona. Here, four water deities symbolize the Danube, Ganges, Nile and Rio de la Plata, while water cascades from their rocky perches.
8. At a distance of about 135 km from Port Blair is Barren Island, which has the only active volcano in India. The island, about 3 km long, has a big crater of the volcano rising abruptly from the sea about half-a-kilometre from the shore and is about 150 fathoms deep.
9. Oceans cover almost three-quarters of the Earth. If all the ice in glaciers and ice sheets melted, the sea level would rise by about 80 metres, about the height of a twenty-six-storey building.
10. The Mercury, Gemini and Apollo spacecraft landed in the Atlantic and Pacific Oceans when they returned to Earth.

GEOGRAPHY-II

1. What is the colour of the disk on the national flag of Bangladesh?
2. Which Indian union territory's roads are based on a unique plan called 7Vs by its original planner?
3. Which is the largest state in terms of area in North-East India?
4. What is the series of concentric coloured arcs that may be seen when light from a distant source—most commonly the Sun—falls upon a collection of water drops called?
5. Name the large island at the southern tip of Italy.
6. In which continent are the Prince Charles Mountains?
7. Traditionally, in which month does the south-west monsoon break in Kerala?
8. Which river is the largest drainage system in the world in terms of the volume of its flow and the area of its basin?
9. Around the Indian Ocean it is referred to as the 'tropical cyclone'; what is it called in North-East Pacific Ocean?
10. Which country's highest peak is Mt. Ararat?

11. Name the only member of the UN whose name begins with the letter 'Q'.
12. Which European country is made up of more than 480 small islands, including the peninsula of Jutland?
13. Which mountains are said to be the backbone of South America?
14. Which famous landmark in Sydney is affectionately nicknamed 'the coat-hanger'?
15. With an average elevation estimated at between 7,000 and 8,000 feet above sea level, which is the world's highest continent?
16. Which word was coined by Rahamat Ali and is said to be an acronym of Punjab, Afgania, Kashmir, Islam or Sind and Balochistan?
17. Dispatched by the *New York Herald* to find David Livingstone, a Scottish missionary who had gone missing in Africa, which river did Henry Morton Stanley find?
18. What is the name of Assam's only hill station?
19. Which European city-state is enclosed within the capital of another country?
20. Which famous landmark would you find between Lake Ontario and Lake Erie?
21. In which city in Europe would you find the Bridge of Sighs?
22. With which European country would you generally associate tulips?
23. Which European country's national symbol is 'The Little Mermaid'?
24. Which is the longest river in Europe?
25. How many capital cities are there in Antarctica?

26. In which country is Bastille Day a national holiday?
27. The name of the main airport of which city was changed from Idlewild to John F. Kennedy?
28. Which two African states merged to form Tanzania?
29. Which is the longest of the five rivers of Punjab?
30. Which country's administrative capital is Sri Jayawardenapura Kotte?
31. Which desert's name means 'great desert' in Mongolian?
32. K2 or Godwin Austen, at 8,610 m, is the world's second highest peak. To which range of mountains does it belong?
33. Which river is known as Jamuna in Bengali and Tsang-po in Tibetan?
34. Which capital city was known to the Romans as 'Lutetia'?
35. Which Asian city was founded by Sir Stamford Raffles in 1819?
36. Which is the only South American country to be bounded by both the Atlantic and Pacific Oceans?
37. What do the following have in common: Anjuna, Baga, Calangute and Miramar?
38. Which Mughal emperor ordered the building of the royal city at Fatehpur Sikri, situated 26 miles west of Agra, Uttar Pradesh?
39. Which was the first comet whose return was predicted, demonstrating that at least some comets are members of the solar system?
40. What geographical feature has the shape of a harp and gets its name from a Greek letter?
41. Which is the world's highest battleground?

42. The Great Sphinx at Giza in Egypt has the head of a man and the body of an animal. What is the animal's name?
43. The Dead Sea lies between Israel and which other country?
44. What is 'the visible discharge of electricity that occurs when a region of a cloud acquires an excess electrical charge, either positive or negative, that is sufficient to break down the resistance of air' called?
45. The name of which ancient city literally means 'the city of cut-stone'?
46. Which country, situated in both Europe and Asia, shares its name with a bird?
47. Gurushikhar is the highest point of the state of…
48. Which present-day Indian city was formerly called Pataliputra, Kusumpura and Azeemabad?
49. In which continent is the Sahara Desert?
50. Which mountain peak is called Chomolungma in Tibetan?

MYTHOLOGY-I

1. In the Mahabharata, what was the name of the only sister of the Kauravas?
2. Which god's tears are believed to be the origin of the rudraksha tree?
3. Which musical instrument does the Hindu goddess of learning hold in her hand?
4. According to the Mahabharata, what did Ekalavya gift as guru dakshina to Dronacharya?
5. Srutakirti was the wife of which son of Dasharatha?
6. In the Mahabharata, who sat at the sleeping Krishna's feet?
7. Which apsara's daughter was Shakuntala?
8. Who was Mandodari's husband?
9. In the Ramayana, who was Bharata's mother?
10. In the Ramayana, who was married to the rakshasa Vidyujjihva?
11. Which Hindu god, known by several names like Amogha, Lalita and Mahisardana, is said to have killed the asura Tarakasura?
12. Which Hindu religious text consists of 1,028 hymns dedicated to various gods?
13. According to Hindu mythology, which incarnation of

Lord Vishnu killed all the male kshatriyas on earth 21 times in succession?

14. In the Mahabharata, which creature did Duryodhana cry like when he was born?
15. Kamban, Krittibas and Tulsidas have all written different versions of which epic?
16. According to Hindu mythology, which is the second of the four yugas?
17. In the Ramayana, what was the name of Rama's only sister?
18. Which sage's hermitage was Shakuntala brought up in?
19. In the Mahabharata, which grandson of Pandu died in warfare when he was surrounded in a 'Chakravyuha'?
20. According to the Ramayana, who founded the city of Ayodhya?
21. In the Mahabharata, Shantanu had two wives: Ganga and…?
22. According to Hindu mythology, who is the king of the yakshas?
23. In Hindu mythology, which deity rides the elephant Airavata?
24. In the Mahabharata, who was known as Gangeya?
25. In the Mahabharata, who taught Bhima the use of the mace?
26. In the Mahabharata, which Pandava was also known as Dhananjaya?
27. In the Mahabharata, what profession did Sahadeva take up in the court of King Virata, while in disguise?
28. In the Ramayana, which rakshasa took the form of a golden deer to lure Lakshmana away, leaving Sita unprotected?

29. Who became the king of Lanka after Ravana was defeated and killed?
30. Which god was the father of Hanuman?
31. In Hindu mythology, what is Lord Vishnu's abode called?
32. In the Mahabharata, who was the commander of the Pandava forces during the battle of Kurukshetra?
33. According to Hindu mythology, what is Agni's vehicle?
34. In the Mahabharata, whose son was Parikshit?
35. In the Mahabharata, Bhishma forcibly abducted three princesses Amba, Ambika and...?
36. In Hindu mythology, what is Lord Krishna's Panchajanya?
37. In Hindu mythology, what kind of an animal is Lord Shiva's Nandi?
38. In Hindu mythology, which deity is also called Mahishasuramardini?
39. Who became the commander of the Kaurava forces after Bhishma retired from the battle?
40. In the Ramayana, who was killed by Lakshmana before he could perform a yagna that would make him invulnerable?
41. What form did Vishnu assume in his seventh avatar?
42. To which god is the sacred Hindu prayer, the Gayatri Mantra, addressed?
43. In the Mahabharata, who among the Pandavas became Uttara's dance teacher at King Virata's palace?
44. Who gave the asuras Sumbha and Nisumbha the boon that their death could only be at the hands of a

woman?
45. In the Mahabharata, who was the eldest son of Kunti?
46. According to Hindu mythology, who killed Shravan Kumar and incurred his father's wrath?
47. Which town was ruled by Kansa?
48. Which god appeared as the emblem on Arjuna's flag?
49. In the Mahabharata, who was cursed for killing Parikshit while he was still in the womb?
50. How do we know Mrigavyadha the dacoit?

Derek's Fun Facts

MYTHOLOGY

1. In the Mahabharata, a fisherman once caught a fish and cut it. He found two human babies in its stomach. He gave the male child to the king. This child later became the Matsya King. The female child was called Matsya-Gandhi meaning 'she who has the smell of fish'; also known as Satyavati.
2. In the Ramayana, Vibhisana reminded Rama and Lakshmana about Brahma's warning that Indrajit could only be killed if his yagna was obstructed. They deliberately went to fight with him when he was performing the yagna for victory over Rama at Nikumbhila. Hearing their words and provoked, Indrajit began fighting without completing the yagna and Lakshmana killed him.
3. In the Ramayana, King Dasaratha divided among his wives the divine pudding got from the 'putrakamesti' yagna, performed so that he might be blessed with children. But a kite snatched away some of it. On its way the pudding fell from its beaks on to the fingers of Anjana doing tapas in the forest. She ate it and Hanuman was born to her.
4. In the Mahabharata, Duryodhana carried away King Virata's cattle. The king was absent from his palace at that time and his son, Prince Uttara, being young did not have the courage to attack Duryodhana. On Panchali's suggestion, Arjuna

in the guise of Brihannala, served as Uttara's charioteer and went with him into battle.
5. In the Mahabharata, when the Pandavas departed on their Mahaprasthana, they handed over the reign of the kingdom to Parikshit, the grandson of Arjuna.
6. In Hindu mythology, the son of Dusyanta and Shakuntala was named Sarvadamana by the sage Kashyapa and later came to be known as Bharata.
7. The Ramayana is considered to be the first poetic composition in the world and hence it is called Adi Kavya.
8. In the Mahabharata, even though King Salya was the brother of Madri and hence the maternal uncle of the Pandavas, yet he fought on the Kaurava's side in the battle of Kurukshetra.
9. In the Mahabharata, Amba ended her life with the vow that she would take revenge on Bhishma and was reborn as Sikhandi, the daughter of King Drupada, and helped Arjuna kill Bhishma in Kurukshetra.
10. In the Ramayana, Dasharatha could ride his chariot in ten different directions.

MYTHOLOGY-II

1. According to Hindu mythology, which god wrote the penal code of the world?
2. Which deity's vahana is a black buffalo?
3. In the Mahabharata, which queen was also known as Prsati because she was the granddaughter of Prasata?
4. Which Pandava was also known as Dhananjaya?
5. After watching Sita apply vermillion to her parting, who applied vermillion over his body to ensure Rama's long life?
6. In the Mahabharata, who had a bow called Vijaya?
7. Which peak of Himavan keeps heaven in its place by supporting it?
8. What forms chapters 25-45 in the Bhisma Parva of the Mahabharata?
9. In Hindu mythology, who were the female equivalent of the Gandharvas?
10. In the Mahabharata, who helped Bhima kill Jarasandha?
11. In the Mahabharata, Vrisaka and Achala were brothers of which important character?
12. In whose palace does Vishwakarma live and serve?
13. Who is Sampati's brother?

14. Which god inspired Valmiki to write the Ramayana?
15. In the Mahabharata, from which element was Draupadi born?
16. Who was married to Satyabhama, Kalindi and Jambavati?
17. In the Ramayana, who lost his strength and vitality due to a curse by the sage Trinabindu?
18. In Hindu mythology, Narada is generally depicted with which musical instrument?
19. In the Mahabharata, who cursed Krishna that he would be killed by trickery?
20. In the Mahabharata, who did Adhiratha rescue from a basket floating down a river?
21. Which collection of stories was written for the sons of King Amarasakti?
22. According to Hindu mythology, who was Prahlad's father?
23. How many brothers did Duryodhana have?
24. In the Mahabharata, which god disguised himself as a dog and went to heaven with Yudhisthira?
25. Which incarnation of Vishnu measured the Three Worlds in three steps?
26. In the Ramayana, Sumitra had two sons, Lakshmana and …
27. Vishnu has two gatekeepers, Jaya and …?
28. According to the Puranas, which continent is India located in?
29. In the Ramayana, which sage taught Rama and Lakshmana all that he knew about weapons?
30. Which Indian epic has a section named Kishkinda Kand?

31. According to Ramayana, which demon was once a god called Jaya?
32. According to Hindu mythology, which king was an incarnation of an asura called Kalanemi?
33. Which god has two wives, Buddhi and Suddhi?
34. According to Hindu mythology, how many heads did Lord Brahma have?
35. Which god's chariot is drawn by seven horses named after the seven Vedic metres?
36. Which of Lord Vishnu's avatars manifested before Prahlada as a result of his devotion?
37. In the Ramayana, who pierced seven trees to prove his bravery to Sugreeva?
38. In the Mahabharata, who kept Arjuna's bow Gandiva for its first thousand years?
39. According to Hindu mythology, what is the last of the seven regions or worlds under the Earth called?
40. In Hindu mythology, who is the guardian of the south-east?
41. When he was born, in which creature's voice did Ashwatthama cry?
42. According to Hindu mythology, gods take three kinds of incarnation: avesa, amsa and …?
43. In the Mahabharata, during the game of dice, who dragged Panchali to the sabha by her hair?
44. Who cursed Kunti that she would not be able to keep a secret?
45. In the Ramayana, what is the name of the ancient kingdom of monkeys?
46. According to Hindu mythology, which type of animal is Kamdhenu?

47. In the Mahabharata, who among the Pandavas was the father of Ghatotkacha?
48. In the Mahabharata, Krishna, Arjuna and Bhima crossed which river on their way to Girivraja from Indraprastha?
49. In Hindu mythology, which god was born as Pradyumna, the son of Krishna and Rukmini?
50. In the Ramayana, whose wife was Sulochana?

SCIENCE-I

1. When Indira Gandhi asked Rakesh Sharma how India appeared from space, what did he say?
2. The Harrier is an example of VTOL aircraft. What does the abbreviation VTOL stand for?
3. Give one word for a code quietly inserted into a computer program and designed to spread through a computer system in order to disrupt and corrupt stored information.
4. What is the temperature at which Fahrenheit and Celsius scales show the same numeric value?
5. Which is the largest joint in the human body?
6. Which is the most widely used of all solvents?
7. A diamond is made up of carbon. Similarly, two precious stones are composed of the same substance, corundum. Name them.
8. Which planet, apart from Venus, rotates east to west?
9. What name is acetylsalicyclic acid better known as?
10. Which famous World War II fighter plane did R.J. Mitchell design in 1936?
11. Which organ of the human body is the word pulmonary connected to?
12. What useful mathematical tool did John Napier devise?

13. The first French space satellite was named after a famous cartoon character. Name the character.
14. Which mode of transport is an original form of the velocipede?
15. In 1696, who was appointed Warden of the Royal Mint, London?
16. What is common to the following terms: beam, arch, cantilever and suspension?
17. Find the odd one out: Pascal, Newton, BASIC, COBOL and ALGOL?
18. What is 'repeated addition' more commonly known as?
19. Which is the closest star to the Earth?
20. Encephalitis is a disease that affects the brain. Which part of your body is affected when you have hepatitis?
21. Which gland swells as a result of goitre?
22. How is muriatic acid better known?
23. Which is the odd one out and why: ringworm, hookworm, tapeworm and roundworm?
24. Other than your head, where will you find a crown in your body?
25. The Penny Black was the first stamp. The Penny Farthing was an earlier type of what? (Hint: It was a means of transport.)
26. A species of which plant is known as prickly pear?
27. Who invented the process of pasteurization?
28. In your body, which are the most active muscles, exercised over 1,00,000 times a day?
29. Which strong, light metal, often used in making aircraft, is named after the mythical first sons of the Earth?

30. What important event took place at the Groote Schuur Hospital, Cape Town, South Africa, on 3 December 1967?
31. Which bodily function is caused by the vibration of the palate by turbulent airflow?
32. What important part did James Phipps play in the history of medicine?
33. What is the geological name of the period of time from 199.6 million to 145.5 million years ago?
34. Which rodent gives its name to a device attached to a computer?
35. If your larynx was removed, what handicap would you suffer from?
36. What is missing in all aphyllous plants?
37. Both a mercury barometer and an aneroid barometer are used to measure pressure. Why is an aneroid barometer so named?
38. Plumbing is the name given to all pipes which carry clean and dirty water in a house. What is the origin of the word?
39. Which two elements were first isolated by Madam Curie from the residue separation of uranium from pitchblende?
40. Give one word for a large collection of information that has been coded and stored in a computer in such a way that it can be extracted under a number of different category headings.
41. After watching steam escape from what did James Watt decide to adapt existing steam engines?
42. In 1979, the World Health Organization declared the world free of this disease. Name it.

43. Which two gases react to give water?
44. Acetic acid is used in the preparation of pickles, confectionery and soft drinks. What is the more common term for it?
45. What is 20/20 vision?
46. What is common to Digger, Prince and Paratrooper?
47. What would you be having checked if a doctor showed you a Snellen's Chart?
48. Which word describes 0.9144 of a metre?
49. What is common to Ed White, Kathy Sullivan and Alexei Leonov?
50. With which numeral does @ share a key on a standard keyboard?

Derek's Fun Facts

SCIENCE

1. The Taj Mahal is being saved from the corrosive effects of industrial pollution by an ancient face-pack recipe, multani mitti (Fuller's earth). According to reports, archaeologists discovered that in the 16th century it was common to use a mud mixture to clean and preserve marble.
2. If we collected the 90 million mobile phones that we no longer use, they could be recycled for the metal inside them. This would equal 18 tonnes of copper, 4,28,000 ounces of silver and 85,000 ounces of gold.
3. After the first powered aircraft, the Wright Flyer, made history at Kitty Hawk, North Carolina in 1903, the Wright brothers disassembled it and shipped it to Dayton, Ohio, where it was stored in a shed behind their bicycle shop for more than a decade.
4. Chandrashekhar Venkata Raman joined the Indian Finance Department in 1907. Though the duties of his office took most of his time, Raman still carried on experimental research in the laboratory of the Indian Association for the Cultivation of Science at Calcutta. He was elected a Fellow of the Royal Society early in his career (1924), and was knighted in 1929. He received the Nobel Prize in Physics in 1930 for the 'Raman Effect', that is, the

change in the wavelength of light that occurs when a light beam is deflected by molecules.
5. Curium was identified by Glenn T. Seaborg and Albert Ghiorso in 1944 and isolated by Isadore Perlman and Louis Werner in 1947. It was named in honour of Pierre and Marie Curie. Minute amounts of curium probably occur naturally in uranium-containing minerals.
6. Twelve astronauts have walked on the moon, collectively them bringing back 382 kilograms of rocks, pebbles, sand and dust.
7. Earth is the only name for a planet of the solar system that does not come from Greco-Roman mythology.
8. Isaac Newton became the Warden and then Master of the Mint in the 1600s and became deeply interested in counterfeiting. He became the terror of London counterfeiters, sending a huge number to the gallows.
9. Because the Moon has only one-sixth the gravity of Earth, you would weigh six times lesser on the Moon than what you weigh on Earth.
10. Photography means 'writing with light'. English astronomer John Herschel, whose father discovered infrared, coined the term.

SCIENCE-II

1. Alessandro Volta invented a stack of copper and zinc disks, with cardboard in salt water to separate them and keep them moist to make a good connection. What had he invented?
2. The Englishman Ralph Wedgwood soaked a thin paper in ink and dried it between sheets of blotting paper. What did he invent?
3. What is common to yellow, scarlet, Q and hay?
4. What would a graphologist study?
5. The adjectives renal and hepatic refer to which part of the human body?
6. The first cervical vertebra in the human body shares its name with which mythological person?
7. Dactyloscopy is the science of identifying what?
8. What is special about a pan coated with teflon?
9. What is the popular name for the third molar in each jaw?
10. What is breakbone fever commonly known as?
11. If the salt you are eating is lacking in 'I', what is it lacking in?
12. The name of this disease comes from a root verb in the Kimakonde language meaning 'to become

contorted' and describes the stooped appearance of sufferers with joint pain. What is its name?
13. Who was the first woman to use the term 'radioactivity'?
14. What should an analgesic kill?
15. Dengue haemorrhagic fever (DHF), a potentially lethal complication, was first recognized in the 1950s during dengue epidemics in the Philippines and which other country?
16. Where may you find the 'Islets of Langerhans'?
17. What follows every action according to Newton's Third Law of Motion?
18. Which natural process gets its name from the Greek words meaning 'light' and 'together'?
19. Name the 1,00,000-odd species of plants which lack chlorophyll.
20. Which family do mint plants belong to?
21. Which part of the body is affected by glaucoma?
22. What was first identified as a new element in 1781, and first isolated as a metal in 1783?
23. Cerebellum and cerebrum are parts of which organ in the human body?
24. Which scientist's incomplete last statement was written to honour Israeli independence day?
25. What does a car's radiator do?
26. Which animals are the source of 99 per cent of human rabies deaths?
27. Which gas forms about 21 percent of the atmosphere in terms of volume?
28. What is the repetition of sound caused by reflection of sound waves called?

29. If a small circle has 360 degrees, how many degrees does a big circle have?
30. Which metal was introduced to the public at the Paris Exposition in 1855?
31. What do you call the measurement of the energy that food provides?
32. In the binary system, which two digits represent all the numbers?
33. Which organ of the human body filters fifty gallons of blood every day?
34. In which country was the chikungunya virus first isolated?
35. 'Richard of York gave battle in vain.' Why might your science teacher ask you to memorize this sentence?
36. If you were in charge of lighting in your school play, which two primary colours would you have to mix to get yellow?
37. The word 'atom' comes from the Greek word atomos. What does it literally mean?
38. The first stanza of which nursery rhyme did Thomas Edison use to test the phonograph he invented in 1877?
39. Which planet has the largest volcano in the solar system?
40. Which organ of the human body forms the widest part of the digestive system?
41. In computer jargon, what does GIGO stand for?
42. Which famous scientist founded the *Indian Journal of Physics* and the Indian Academy of Sciences and trained hundreds of students?
43. Patients belonging to which blood group are said to be 'universal receivers'?

44. What conversion can be made by subtracting 32, multiplying by 5 and dividing by 9?
45. The literal meaning of this word is 'belly speaking'. How is it better known?
46. When its height is three quarters to its depth, what is said to build up and break?
47. Whose laboratory assistant was Thomas Watson?
48. Fill in the blank: the wheel and axle, the lever, the ramp, the screw and the pulley are all_____machines.
49. Which gas gives Uranus its distinctive blue-green colour?
50. Who named his first work on arithmetic after his daughter Lilavati in order to console her?

INDIA-I

1. Which patriotic song is also known as *Tarana-e-Hindi* or the 'Song of the Indian'?
2. The wood for which festival is customarily brought from the ex-princely state of Dasapalla, by a specialist team of carpenters who have hereditary rights and privilege for the same?
3. In 1591, which monument was constructed in Hyderabad to commemorate the end of a plague epidemic?
4. Which Indian monument did Rabindranath Tagore describe as 'a teardrop on the face of eternity'?
5. Which mode of transport, commonly known as 'streetcars', was discontinued in Chennai in 1953?
6. According to the Saka calendar, which is the first month?
7. What is the name of the first Indian-made nuclear submarine?
8. Which cartoonist would you associate with the *You Said It* series?
9. What was unique about the composition of the 88th Battalion of CRPF, formed in the early 1990s?
10. Name the well-known Indian occupant of the

spacecraft Soyuz T-11, between April 3-11, 1984.
11. Which Indian state is the popular dish sorpotel from?
12. What are the two words inscribed on the national emblem of India?
13. Three cities in India are considered as part of the 'Golden Triangle' tour by tour operators. If Delhi and Agra are two, which is the third?
14. *Something Beautiful for God* is a book by Malcolm Muggeridge. Who is the subject of the book?
15. Pingalli Venkayya is credited with designing which national symbol of India?
16. By what name are the National Security Guards better known?
17. Which Indian organization's motto is 'Unity and Discipline'?
18. In which city can you visit the famous Kite Museum designed by Bhanu Shah?
19. Which IIT started its journey in the old Hijli Detention Camp where some of our great freedom fighters toiled and sacrificed their lives for the independence of our country?
20. What was adopted on 26 November 1949, but came into effect on 26 January 1950?
21. Who was the founder of Banaras Hindu University?
22. In 1661, which city was presented to King Charles II as part of the dowry when he married Princess Catherine de Braganza of Portugal?
23. Which Indian state capital begins and ends with the letter 'A'?
24. In West India, what would you do with a 'pao'?
25. Built by King Narasimhadeva in the thirteenth

century, what was designed in the shape of a colossal chariot with seven horses and twenty-four wheels?
26. What are referred to as 'kabbas' at the Karni Mata temple at Deshnok?
27. In North India, which musical instrument is also known as venu, vamsi and murali?
28. In 1993, the winner of this contest was Dayanara Torres. Who won it in 1994?
29. In 1998, India conducted nuclear tests at Pokhran. Which was the site for the 1974 set of tests?
30. The Republic Day parade in New Delhi starts near Rashtrapati Bhawan and ends at...
31. Which Indian musician's autobiography is *Raga Mala*?
32. In which field of art did Manjit Bawa attain fame?
33. With which Pandava does the 'Father of the Indian Constitution' share his name?
34. Which India organization's motto is 'Duty Unto Death'?
35. If you visited 'Arjuna's Penance', in which temple town would you be?
36. Which city in North-Eastern India was once known as Pragjyotishpura (the light of the East)?
37. What was set up as an Armed Force of the Union in 1978 on recommendations of the Rustamji Committee for preservation and protection of our Exclusive Economic Zone (EEZ)?
38. In which state of India did calico, the all-cotton fabric, originate?
39. In 1973, which environmental movement started when the women of Uttar Pradesh, under the leadership of Chandi Prasad Bhatt, went into the forest and formed

a circle around the trees preventing men from cutting them down?
40. The fourteen coaches of which luxury train are named after former Rajput states?
41. In India, which capital city was planned by Vidyadhar Bhattacharya?
42. Which colour occupies the least space on the national flag of India?
43. Which Indian military medal features the vajra of Indra?
44. In which Indian city is the National Rail Museum located?
45. In the 1800s, the 'Victoria Portrait' series was the first set of British Indian . . .
46. Which part of the Indian armed forces has squadrons named Black Panthers, Sharks and Rhinos?
47. By what name is the famous Samantik Mani now known?
48. Which item of clothing is worn in Nivi, Gujarati and Gond styles?
49. Which festival connects Magh, Kati and Bohag?
50. Which is independent India's first multi-purpose river-valley project?

Derek's Fun Facts

INDIA

1. India is the only country that produces all the varieties of silk.
2. Traditionally, Indian money has enjoyed wide circulation in the Persian Gulf region. Between 1959 and 1966 India issued notes for circulation in the Persian Gulf region as well as special notes for Haj pilgrims.
3. The last of the British ships that set sail for England after the independence of India left from the Gateway of India.
4. Held annually, the culural, trade-cum-religious Pushkar Fair is also among the largest cattle fairs of the world.
5. Shingnapur, a village under Newasa Taluka of Ahmednagar district in Maharashtra, has a temple of Lord Saturn (Shani) and is a pilgrimage centre. For generations together, the houses there do not have doors. They keep their belongings in the open.
6. The national flag is said to have been first hoisted in India on 7 August 1906, in the Parsee Bagan Square (Green Park) in Calcutta. The flag was composed of three horizontal strips of red, yellow and green.
7. The Gol Gumbaz at Bijapur has a 'Whispering Gallery', where even a single loud clap is distinctly echoed over ten times.

8. The Lifeline Express, also known as the Jeevan Rekha Express, is believed to be the world's first hospital on a train. The train, which is the flagship of Impact India Foundation, in partnership with the Indian Railways, has medically served more than 7,00,000 people in rural India.
9. Nawab Wajid Ali Shah of Avadh composed a number of songs and plays under the pen name Akhtari Pia.
10. Before the creation of Chhattisgarh, Madhya Pradesh was the largest state in India in terms of area.

INDIA-II

1. Which sect, established by Swami Jambeshwar Maharaj, is named after the twenty-nine tenets laid down by him?
2. Which mountain is honoured in the festival of Pang Lhabsol celebrated in Sikkim?
3. By what name is the Baha'i Temple in New Delhi popularly known?
4. In 1992, which country was granted the Teen Bigha corridor by India?
5. If you were making a terracota flower vase, what would you use as a base ingredient?
6. In Jammu and Kashmir, which craft is referred to as 'kari kamandari'?
7. Which industrialist was awarded the United Nations Population Award in 1992?
8. Which Indian state attained statehood after 451 years of colonial rule and twenty-six years as a union territory?
9. The raga Bilaskhani Todi was created by Bilas Khan. Whose son was Bilas Khan?
10. Who was the first musician to receive the Bharat Ratna?
11. The Pattamadai mats are a speciality of which South Indian state?

12. Which Indian percussion instrument's name literally means 'body of clay'?
13. Which musical instrument was referred to as 'Shata-tantri-veena' in ancient times?
14. Who said, 'Ravi Shankar is the godfather of world music'?
15. The dish 'Junglee maas' is a unique creation of a maharaja of which state?
16. By what name is 'dalchini' known in English?
17. What was hailed as 'Britain's true national dish' by Foreign Secretary Robin Cook?
18. Which fruit is 'Yubi Lakpi', a traditional game of Manipur, played with?
19. What would you see on the reverse side of a contemporary 50-rupee note?
20. What does the Mysore Paints and Varnish Limited (MPVL) provide during an election?
21. Kuchipudi is indigenous to the state of…
22. Fill in the blank to complete this phrase coined by Sundarlal Bahuguna during the Chipko Movement: 'Ecology is permanent _____'.
23. On which item of daily use do we find the pledge beginning with: 'I promise to pay the bearer the sum of…'?
24. The Bharat Ratna award is designed in the shape of which leaf?
25. In 1926, who founded an ashram with the help of his spiritual collaborator, the Mother?
26. Which social reformer's first two names are Murlidhar Devidas?

27. Who set up a dance school called Nrityagram near Bengaluru?
28. Who was the first woman to feature on an Indian stamp?
29. Who composed the lyrics of the song 'Sare Jahan Se Achcha'?
30. Which lighting device does Bholu, the mascot of Indian Railways, hold in his hand?
31. Which is the oldest functioning steam locomotive in the world?
32. Which style of folk painting is referred to as 'Mithila Art'?
33. In Rajasthan, what is normally eaten with bati and churma?
34. Which national park was established as Hailey National Park in 1935?
35. Which Bharat Ratna recipient's father was a court musician in the princely state of Dumraon in Bihar?
36. This railway station in Mumbai was formerly known as Victoria Terminus. How do we know it today?
37. Which is India's first planned industrial city?
38. In India, what does PNR on a railway ticket stand for?
39. Which style of painting shares its name with the largest tribe of northern Mumbai?
40. What took place in India for the first time on 7 July 1896 at Watson's Hotel in Mumbai?
41. According to the state emblem of India, which animal is the guardian of the east?
42. Before independence, it was known as the Crown Representative's Police. How do we know it today?
43. Which country is the second largest producer of silk in the world?

44. The Pattachitra style of painting is one of the oldest and most popular art forms of India. Which state is it from?
45. Which Indian capital town's name means 'wood' in Portuguese?
46. Where is the Kumbh Mela held in Maharashtra?
47. If you were at the holy Dasashwamedh and Manikarnika ghats, which city would you be in?
48. Which national symbol can only be made using hand spun and hand woven wool/cotton/silk khadi bunting?
49. The words 'Satyameva Jayate' on the national emblem of India are taken from which Upanishad?
50. The word 'Dachigam' in the name Dachigam National Park refers to a particular number in a language. Which number?

WILDLIFE-I

1. What do you call a male horse that is less than four years old?
2. What are 'brood parasites'?
3. Which species of apes have the longest tails on reaching adulthood?
4. Barking, swamp, musk and rein are all types of an animal. Name it.
5. Which is the first animal you come across when you go through a dictionary?
6. What is the common name for the small reddish-golden Eurasian carp normally kept as a pet at home?
7. What is common to Siberian, Bengal and Sumatran?
8. After which land animal is the largest species of seal named?
9. A young cow is called a calf. What is a young rhino called?
10. The Indian grey species of which cat-like carnivore is capable of killing venomous snakes?
11. Only one forest is home to the Asiatic lion. Name it.
12. Which carnivorous mammal, found in the Himalayan range, is also called ounce?
13. In a colony of bees, what are male bees called?

14. Which is the only snake to build a nest for its eggs?
15. Which Indian state is the Dachigam National Park situated in?
16. The age of a tree can be estimated by counting the rings. How can you tell the age of a horse?
17. The Komodo Dragon is the largest variety of a creature. Name it.
18. A tigon is an offspring of a tiger and a lioness. What do you call the offspring of a lion and a tigress?
19. Which animal's name originates from the Old Norse word 'hrosshvalr', which means 'horse whale'?
20. The duckbilled platypus and the echidna or the anteater are the only two mammals to do what?
21. What animal is represented by the following types: Siamese, Persian, Caffre?
22. A rabbit's tail is called a scut. What is a fox's tail called?
23. How is 'bluebuck' commonly known in India?
24. What is the more common name for 'Bovine spongiform encephalopathy'?
25. The ostrich is the world's largest bird. Which is the second largest living bird?
26. In India, it is called bhalu. How is it known in the West?
27. In which part of a butterfly's body is its sense of taste located?
28. What is the correct name for a baby wombat?
29. Which term was coined in 1842 by the English paleontologist Richard Owen?
30. Which are the only cats that live in groups called prides?

31. What do baby whales feed on?
32. How many miles can a full-grown ostrich fly?
33. What is North America's largest rodent?
34. How many stomachs does a cow have?
35. In which country is the Morton National Park located?
36. Which present-day animal did the prehistoric mammoth closely represent?
37. Which five-letter word is the name for an American buffalo?
38. Which animal's name was adopted as a nickname or mascot by a number of South African sports teams?
39. Which two things do bees collect?
40. Name a microscopic single-celled animal beginning and ending with the same letter.
41. Which breed of dog is also called the Congo bush dog?
42. What averages 30 per minute in elephants and 400 per minute in chicks?
43. Which is the state bird of Odisha?
44. Which animal is called Ora or the 'land crocodile', by the inhabitants of the island where this animal dwells?
45. Which animal species is the world's largest terrestrial animal?
46. Which insect is nicknamed 'devil's darning needle'?
47. Which is the closest relative of the okapi, a cud-chewing hoofed mammal found in the rainforests of Congo and in zoos around the world?
48. Which animal, the largest land carnivore, is reputed to be the only animal that actively hunts human?

49. Which animal is often known as Elite Arab?
50. Which animal's largest species is represented by the Conraua goliath?

Derek's Fun Facts

WILDLIFE

1. Each tiger has its very own stripe pattern. Other interesting tiger markings are the white spots on the backs of their ears. This may be a visual cue for tigers looking for other tigers, or it may be a way for mothers to keep track of their cubs in the dense forest undergrowth.
2. An ostrich's eye is almost 2 inches across, the largest eye of any land animal. Ostriches eat things that other animals can't digest. They have tough intestines that are 46 feet long. These big birds also swallow sand, pebbles and small stones that help grind up food in the gizzard.
3. The tallest living tree is a Coast Redwood known as the 'Mendocino Tree' found in Montgomery State Reserve in California. This tree, which is over 1,000 years old, is more than 367 feet and 6 inches tall and is still growing.
4. The Great Banyan Tree (*Ficus bengalensis*) of the Indian Botanic Garden, Kolkata attracts millions of visitors every year. It looks like a miniature forest and is over 250 years old with 2,800 prop roots covering an area of 1.5 hectares.
5. Dame Jane Morris Goodall is a British primatologist, anthropologist and UN Messenger of Peace. Goodall is best known for her forty-five-year study of social and family interactions of wild chimpanzees

in Gombe Stream National Park, Tanzania. She is the founder of the Jane Goodall Institute and has worked extensively on conservation and animal welfare issues.

6. You can tell the temperature by listening to the chirping of a cricket. The frequency of chirping varies according to temperature. To get a rough estimate of the temperature in degrees Fahrenheit, count the number of chirps in 15 seconds and then add 37. The number you get will be an approximation of the temperature outside.

7. Adélie penguins were named by the French explorer Dumont d'Urville. He named them after his wife, whose name was Adélie.

8. The fur of a polar bear looks white because the air spaces in each hair scatter light of all colors. The color white becomes visible to our eyes when an object reflects back all of the visible wavelengths of light, rather than absorbing some of the wavelengths.

9. The largest turtle is the leatherback turtle. The length of its shell can be up to 8 feet (2.4 metres) and the smallest is the bog turtle. Many aquatic turtles like the matamata use the 'gape and suck' method to eat. They lie in wait for a fish, then suddenly open their mouths wide and expand their throats, which suck in the fish.

10. A teaspoon of sea water can contain as many as a million one-celled phytoplankton.

WILDLIFE-II

1. The dhole is a species of an animal family. Name it.
2. The white-backed, long-billed and slender-billed are species of a bird of prey. Which bird is it?
3. Among land vertebrates, which bird has the largest eyes?
4. Which feature's modified forms are the 'teeth' on the snout of a sawfish?
5. Which Himalayan animal is also called *kasturi mriga* in Hindi?
6. In 2006, which animal's natural habitat in China became a UNESCO World Heritage site?
7. Which is the only species of snake found inside the Arctic Circle?
8. Which bird's scientific name is *Struthio camelus*, meaning camel-like, as it makes its own water internally and gets the rest from vegetation?
9. How many arms does a starfish normally have?
10. What is a group of baboons collectively called?
11. Which mammal found in the Arctic Circle uses its extremely sensitive whiskers, called mustacial vibrissae, as detection devices?
12. Which Indian state has adopted the sangai, a type of brow-antlered deer, as its state animal?

13. Which creature gets its name from the colour of the lining of its mouth, which is purple-black, and which it displays when threatened?
14. Which is the loudest insect in the world?
15. Which national park in Assam is known as Mini Kaziranga?
16. For which animal did Constantine John Phipps choose the scientific name *Ursus maritimus*, the Latin for 'maritime bear'?
17. Which breed of dog is named after a nomadic tribe in Maharashtra?
18. If you saw the endangered 'khur' in Gujarat, which animal would you have seen?
19. Which is the only state in India to have more than one reserved forest included in the UNESCO World Heritage sites list?
20. Which animal dies of malnutrition when its last molar is worn out?
21. The name of which member of the cat family comes from a Native American word meaning 'he who kills with one leap'?
22. Which animal's conservation did Canada, Denmark, Norway, USA and the former USSR sign an agreement for in Oslo on 15 November 1973?
23. Which fox's greyish-yellow coat turns into a different colour for a part of the year?
24. Which creature, found in the River Ganges, is also known as 'susu'?
25. Which animal's upper incisors are the longest and heaviest?

26. Which animal's first captive-breeding centre is in the Nandan Kanan Wildlife Sanctuary in Odisha?
27. Periwinkles and queen conchs are the names of the species of a creature. Name it.
28. What kind of animal is the *kulan*, generally found in the Gobi Desert?
29. Which reptile outlives all other vertebrates, including man?
30. Which is the only continent where owls are not found in the wild?
31. Which bird's varieties are the ivory-billed, the acorn and the great-spotted?
32. Which animal's extinct subspecies are Javan, Bali and Caspian?
33. Which animal's smallest specimen is pudu?
34. Which breed of dog was originally developed in Germany to hunt badgers?
35. Which insect is also known as angleworm since it is used as fish bait?
36. Which bird has the longest wingspan in the bird kingdom—up to 11 feet (3.4 meters)?
37. Which are the only cats to have a tuft or a bunch of hair at the end of their tail?
38. Which is the only spiny mammal found in its natural habitat in Britain?
39. Which is the only member of the cat family that hunts primarily during the day?
40. What do Adelie penguins use to mark out their nests?
41. What is the colour of the eyes of a Cactus Ferruginous Pygmy Owl?

42. Which bird's varieties would Harpy, Golden, Bald and Sea be?
43. Which animal's smallest species would be the Pygmy Marmoset?
44. Which species of reptiles lay eggs in large numbers at the Gahirmatha Wildlife Sanctuary?
45. A species of which marine creature is thought to be the most intelligent of all invertebrate animals?
46. Which tropical spider's name is derived from that of the Italian seaport of Taranto?
47. The oryx lives in herds in deserts and the dry plains of Africa and Arabia. What type of creature is it?
48. Which burrowing carnivore is closely related to the mongoose?
49. Which animal was unknown to the western world until 1869, when the skin of this animal was found by a French missionary?
50. Which national park contains the world's largest area of mangrove forests?

SPORTS-I

1. What is the post box number of the Australian Broadcasting Corporation, created as a tribute to Don Bradman's batting average?
2. Which Indian game, literally meaning 'four parts of the army', consisted of horses, elephants and foot soldiers?
3. Which sportsman starred in the films *Freedom Road* and *The Greatest*?
4. Which indoor game is often called the 'Hungarian Horror'?
5. Who once scored 36 not out after batting through 60 overs in a World Cup match?
6. Who was the first person to win the Dronacharya Award in athletics?
7. At the 1992 Barcelona Olympic Games, why were coconut shells imported from India?
8. In 1896, Spyridon Louis became the first Greek athlete to win a gold medal in which discipline of athletics?
9. The Chennai suburbs of Vyasapardi, Pulianthope, Periamet, Washermenpet, Tondiarpet and Chintadripet have produced national and world champions in which sport?

10. Who was the first unseeded player to win the Wimbledon Men's Single's title?
11. Which famous Hungarian international footballer was known as the 'Galloping Major'?
12. If someone was participating in 'Le Mans', which sport would he be an expert in?
13. In athletics, over how many days is the decathlon played?
14. Which Indian athlete was known as the 'Payyoli Express'?
15. After which bird was the Spanish footballer Emilio Butragueno nicknamed?
16. Who was the first batsman in the history of international cricket to be given out by the third umpire?
17. My father was a hockey Olympian. My mother was a basketball player of repute. I, too, am a famous Indian sportsman. Who am I?
18. If Wimbledon is played on grass, which tournament is played on Deco Turf II?
19. In Indian football, if 'Red and Gold' is playing against 'Maroon and Green', then which two teams are playing?
20. The first Indian Chess Grandmaster is Vishwanathan Anand. Who is the second?
21. From which island did the three W's of West Indian cricket (Weekes, Worrell and Walcott) come?
22. How many holes would you have played if you played 'a complete round of golf'?
23. What sport would you be good at if you represent your school in the Subroto Mukherji Cup?

24. Which former cricketer was nicknamed the 'Super Cat' or the 'Big Cat'?
25. Which form of intimidatory bowling was banned in cricket after 1933?
26. Before the 'hit-off' regulation, how did a hockey match start?
27. Which sport did all these people excel in: George Hackenschmidt, the Great Gama, Ed Lewis and Frank Gotch?
28. The scoring system for which sport originated from the positions of the hands of a clock?
29. Who was the first Indian to captain the Oxford University cricket team?
30. Which was the first sporting event to be broadcast live on television?
31. The contingent of which country marches last in the Olympic march past?
32. For which athletic event did Dick Fosbury invent a new technique and greatly influence the sport?
33. Which sportsman was nicknamed 'The Louisville Lip' because of the way he used to boast before a contest?
34. Which African dictator was also his country's light heavyweight boxing champion?
35. What are the two categories in the diving events at the Olympic Games?
36. Which Indian cricketer named his son after Sunil Gavaskar and footballer Inder Singh?
37. Which US tennis star is believed to have popularised the two-handed backhand return?
38. The World Cup Football finals of 1970 and 1986 were played in the same stadium. Name the stadium.

39. Usually, what colours are present in the chequered flag waved at the end of motor races?
40. What is given every year to Europe's leading goal scorer in football?
41. Name the racquet sport which gets its name from the resilience of its balls.
42. In Melbourne, what is affectionately known as the 'G'?
43. If Leander Paes is called Lee, what is Mahesh Bhupathi called?
44. Former cricket umpire Dickie Bird used to wear a cap which was not a cricket cap. Which sport did it belong to?
45. Which is the most prestigious badminton tournament in the UK?
46. After which cricketer is the stadium at St. John's Wood named?
47. Which extremely fast game starts with a face-off?
48. To what does the following routine apply: reach-throw-wide-row-swim-tow and carry?
49. What do you call 'a cheer in a sports stadium that ripples around the crowd'?
50. Which team has won the Indian National Men's Football Championship or the Santosh Trophy the most number of times?

Derek's Fun Facts

SPORTS

1. In 1932, Hugh Buggy, a reporter for *Melbourne Age*, was a few dollars short, so while sending a telegram to his sub-editor, as a substitute for 'in the line of the body' he used the word 'bodyline' to keep the cost down, thus establishing a new term in cricket.
2. In 1966, during the FIFA World Cup, the Chairman of the FIFA Referees' Committee Ken Aston, was driving back to his home after a meeting. While at a traffic signal, stopping at the red light, the idea of cards came to his mind. The concept came into use at the 1970 FIFA World Cup.
3. A children's game, 'Duck on a Rock', was converted into basketball by YMCA instructor James Naismith in 1891, so that the school students would not need to go outdoors to play in the harsh winters of Massachussets, USA.
4. It was a case of a baby swap that was noticed by Madhav Mantri, a former Indian cricketer, who rightly identified his new-born nephew from that of a fisherman's baby. A few decades after that, the nephew created cricketing history. The famous nephew is Sunil Gavaskar.
5. The 1900 Olympic Games were held in Paris as part of the World's Fair. The organizers spread the competitions over five months and under-promoted

their Olympic status to such an extent that many athletes never knew they had actually participated in the Olympic Games.
6. Durand Cup is the third oldest football tournament in the world and the oldest in Asia and India. It was started at Simla in the year 1888 by Sir Henry Mortimer Durand, who was then the Foreign Secretary to the Government of India. The tournament is also unique because the winning team walks away with three trophies. The Durand Cup and Simla Trophy are rolling trophies while the President's Cup first presented by Dr Rajendra Prasad is given to the team permanently.
7. Art competitions were first included on the programme of the Olympic Games in Stockholm in 1912. Though the 1912 contests among painters, sculptors, architects, musicians, and writers were only a modest success, they represented the beginning of a tradition that lasted until the 1948 Olympic Games.
8. In an international football match, all items of jewellery (necklaces, rings, bracelets, earrings, leather bands, rubber bands etc.) are strictly forbidden and must be removed. Using tape to cover jewellery is not acceptable. Referees are also prohibited from wearing jewellery (except for a watch or similar device for timing the match).
9. At fifteen, Sachin Tendulkar scored an unbeaten century against Gujarat at the Wankhede Stadium to become the youngest Indian to make a hundred

on first-class debut. He was picked after Bombay captain Dilip Vengsarkar watched him negotiate Kapil Dev in the nets.

10. The first father-son pair of Indian sportspersons winning medals in different sports in Olympics is the Vece Paes and Leander Paes duo. While Vece Paes was a member of the 1972 bronze-winning Indian hockey team, Leander won the bronze medal in Men's Singles Tennis in 1996, at Atlanta, USA.

SPORTS-II

1. Which country leads the march past in both the Summer and the Winter Olympic Games?
2. What does the nickname 'Perola Negra', often ascribed to Pele, mean?
3. According to the rules, how many players are required on each side to play a game of beach volleyball?
4. In which Olympic sport, Korean in origin, do contestants wear a body guard marked with red and blue areas and score points by striking an opponent in these coloured areas?
5. Who was the first Indian woman to be ranked the junior world number one squash player?
6. Which left-handed batsman published the autobiography, *With Time to Spare*?
7. In which event did Mohini Bharadwaj, representing USA, win a silver medal at the 2004 Athens Olympics?
8. Which Olympic discipline do track, road and mountain come under?
9. What is the longest running race on a track at the Olympic Games?
10. Which former Pakistani pace bowler was nicknamed the 'Burewala Express' in his playing days?

11. Which Indian had the honour of bowling the first ball in the history of Cricket World Cup?
12. Which country's football team is sometimes called the 'socceroos'?
13. Which game is said to be invented by William G. Morgan while he was the physical director of the YMCA in Holyoke, Massachusetts?
14. Since 1992, which team has won the most number of English Premier League titles?
15. Whose record did Mohammed Ashraful break in 2001 when he became the youngest player to score a Test century?
16. Harsh Mankad represented India in tennis. In which sport did his father Ashok Mankad represent India?
17. Whom did Han Jian lose to at the 1981 World Cup Badminton final at Kuala Lumpur?
18. In which sport was Jan-Ove Waldner a double world champion?
19. Who was the first Indian batsman to wear a helmet?
20. Asian Games: which is the only city where India has won a gold medal in hockey?
21. Who was the first Indian to win the World Amateur Snooker Championship?
22. Which European soccer club's home is the Nou Camp Stadium?
23. Which West Indian cricketer's daughter is named after the Australian city Sydney?
24. Which team did the Indian women's cricket team play its first Test match against?
25. In which game is the term 'fluke' used?

26. Among Sri Lankans, who has scored the most number of double hundreds in Test cricket?
27. Which team defeated Australia in their debut match at the 1983 Cricket World Cup?
28. Which Canada-born tennis player resides at Sarasota, USA?
29. Which Olympic sport has events named International Tornado and Flying Dutchman?
30. Whose wicket did Harbhajan Singh take to complete his hat-trick against Australia in 2000-01?
31. Which sport's name has been attributed to the French word meaning 'shepherd's crook'?
32. Who was the first player to play in three successive football World Cup finals?
33. What does USA not do during the march past at the opening ceremony of the Olympic Games that all other countries do?
34. While we have the bicycle kick in football, in which sport would you come across the 'dolphin kick'?
35. Which game can be played on three different mounts: horse, cycle and elephant?
36. Which tennis player won the first 'Golden Slam' in the history of tennis?
37. In 1993, after which Indian cricketers were wards in Tihar Jail named?
38. *Beyond 10,000: My Life Story* is the story of which sportsman?
39. Grandmaster is the highest classification for a chess player. What is the classification immediately below that called?
40. Which German footballer is credited with inventing

the 'attacking sweeper' position?
41. In *Alice's Adventures in Wonderland*, which game was played by the Queen of Hearts using hedgehogs as balls?
42. Who was the first male gymnast to obtain a perfect 10 score at the Olympics?
43. Which football combination is called the 'Christmas Tree' formation?
44. Which word connects a wrestling term and a place where garments are put to dry?
45. Swimming, running and which other event comprise the triathlon?
46. In which sport would you meet a rikishi (or a 'strong man')?
47. Which English football club is sometimes called the 'Gunners'?
48. Which famous cricket event's name stems from an epitaph published after Australia's first win over England in England?
49. In the 20th century, which athlete had the maximum number of world records under his belt?
50. Other than cricket, which is the only outdoor sport in which runs can be scored?

MIXED BAG-I

1. Whose birthday is observed as Teachers' Day in Taiwan?
2. What are electronic, pin-pallet and self-winding different varieties of?
3. The Schengen Visa would enable you to visit the member countries of which organization?
4. Alphabetically, which is the first country listed in the United Nations?
5. Scarlet, crimson and vermillion are shades of which colour?
6. After which famous artist is the airport in Rome named?
7. What does 'D' in the degree D. Litt. stand for?
8. In the Batik method of dyeing, patterned parts are traditionally covered with a substance so that they do not receive colour. What is it?
9. What is prepared by steeping the leaves and leaf buds of the plant Camellia Sinensis in boiling water?
10. What is described in the Oxford Dictionary as 'a black powder used in South Asia as a cosmetic, either around the eyes or as a mark on the forehead'?
11. In astronomy, the name of which zodiacal constellation comes from the Latin word for 'balance'?

12. Which safety device are Barron, Yale and combination types of?
13. On whose behalf did Alexander and Kim Aris accept the Nobel Peace Prize for 1991?
14. With which everyday object would you associate King Gillette?
15. Which island in the South East Pacific is famous for large statues called *moai*?
16. Which fabric was introduced by Sir H.B. Lumsden and W. Hodson in 1848 for British colonial troops in India?
17. In Sri Lanka, it is called Rupavahini. How do we know it in India?
18. Which part of the human body features on the flag of 'Isle of Man'?
19. Which kind of sewing technique comes from the French word meaning 'to put on'?
20. The president of which country is the only non-Indian head of state to receive the Bharat Ratna?
21. The constitution of which country came into force on 16 December 1972?
22. On a standard computer keyboard, which number key features the percentage sign?
23. In the abbreviation ATM, what does 'M' stand for?
24. In comics, by what name is Diana Palmer's husband better known?
25. What do the thirteen stripes on the flag of the US signify?
26. On a Scrabble board, what is the colour of a triple word score?
27. Which temple was formerly known as the 'Black Pagoda'?

28. The tip, shank, spreader ribs and handle are all parts of which everyday object?
29. In an airport, what name is given to a strip of hard ground along which aircraft take off and land?
30. Which sign of the zodiac has a water bearer as its symbol?
31. The black variety of which spice did Europeans refer to as 'Black Gold'?
32. If you wanted to visit the Black Forest, which country would you be in?
33. Between 1977 and 2011, the flag of which country was only green in colour?
34. What did Rudyard Kipling describe as 'a river of life as nowhere else exists in the world'?
35. Who was the famous brother of Vijayalakshmi Pandit?
36. Pigeon-blood red is the most valuable variety of a gemstone. Name the gemstone.
37. In Arab countries, what is a souk?
38. What, when simply numbered, do these three numbers have in common: 11, 69 and 88?
39. 'I swear by Apollo, the healer, by Aesculapius, by Hygeia and all the powers of healing...' Which oath begins with these words?
40. In which country is Sagarmatha National Park located?
41. Which continent did a total of 22,122 tourists visit in 2011-12?
42. Which is the most widely grown cereal in the world?
43. Which country issued the first silk stamp?
44. In Arab countries, which beverage is prepared in an ibriq, and traditionally boiled three times?

45. The name of a popular Indian dish is similar to that of a type of comb for horses, a leaf and a plant. (Hint: five-letter answer). Name it
46. King Cyrus of Persia is reputed to have wished for as many good generals as there are seeds in this fruit. Which fruit?
47. The scientific name of this crop is *Oryza sativa*. About 95 per cent of it is eaten by humans. Name it.
48. Which country is the largest producer of milk in the world?
49. What is common to Dasher, Dancer, Prancer, Vixen, Comet, Cupid, Donner, Biltzen and Rudolph?
50. Almost every village in Thailand has a 'wat'. A wat is a…

Derek's Fun Facts

MIXED BAG

1. British stamps are the only stamps in the world that don't have the country of origin printed on them. They simply display the reigning monarch's head. This is because Britain was the first country in the world to issue stamps in 1840.
2. Data from satellite instruments is also used by fishermen to find areas where fish are most likely to be found.
3. The term 'aeronautics' originated in France, and was derived from the Greek words for 'air' and 'to sail'.
4. Less than three per cent of all water on Earth is freshwater (usable for drinking) and of that amount, more than two-thirds is locked up in ice caps and glaciers.
5. The Central government spent quite a large sum of money over the years on legal requirements to protect the 'Darjeeling tea' brand globally. The tea, produced in the Darjeeling hills of West Bengal, was the first product to be registered in the country under the Geographical Indications of Goods (Registration and Protection) Act, 1999.
6. In 1905, when the British rulers wanted to divide the province of Bengal, Rabindranath Tagore provided a defiant force for the anti-partition movement. He organized 'Raksha Bandhan' on the

day of the proclamation of the partition. The thread-tying ceremony was conducted between Hindus and Muslims as a gesture of religious fraternity and to unite themselves against the foreign rulers' attempt to 'divide and rule'.

7. Lieutenant Burnes in his memoirs describes this region as 'a space without a counterpart in the globe'. Experts have pointed out that even the mirage in the Rann is different, the action of the sun on saline particles somehow working differently here. Like an endless, dried up sea, the Rann of Kutch stretches over 23,000 square kilometres of area, where neither herb nor forage nor tree is to be seen for miles on end.

8. On 25 August 1932, Amelia Earhart set three records for women flyers: the first non-stop US crossing, the longest distance record, and a coast-to-coast record time.

9. Graphite was discovered near Keswick, England, in the mid-16th century. A.G. Werner, an 18th-century German chemist, called it graphite from the Greek *graphein*, 'to write'.

10. The paper used for US bills isn't made from trees. Rather, it contains 75 per cent cotton and 25 per cent linen.

MIXED BAG-II

1. The name of which spice comes from the French word for 'nail of gillyflower'?
2. Normally, which letter of the alphabet has the least number of entries in an English dictionary?
3. Which puzzle's name is the Japanese abbreviation of a phrase, meaning 'the digits must occur only once'?
4. Which crop is sometimes referred to as 'white gold'?
5. In which category have the maximum number of women won the Nobel Prize?
6. Which colour is common to the national flags of Nepal and India?
7. Which Greek letter was the Euro symbol inspired by?
8. Which accessory has parts called the circle, or hoop; the shoulders; and the bezel?
9. What is the brimless, cone-shaped hat that was abolished as part of the Turkish national dress in 1925 called?
10. Which tree's leaves appear on the flag of the United Nations?
11. In which part of the body would you wear Oxfords and Jodhpurs?
12. Which sign on a computer keyboard is generally called 'Affenschwanz' or 'monkey's tail' in German?

13. What constitutes 90 per cent of the weight of commercially produced mushrooms?
14. In an English dictionary, the names of how many days of the week start with 'T'?
15. Who was the first person to climb all fourteen of the world's highest mountains?
16. With which international organization would you associate the 'World Jamboree'?
17. Whose portrait does the stamp Penny Black depict?
18. About 70 per cent of all the home pages on the Internet are in which language?
19. Which is the most frequently shown flower on the Sanchi Stupa?
20. What is the full form of SMS?
21. If '.in' is the Internet code of India, then '.zm' is the Internet code of which country?
22. The name of which food item is thought to have come from the Chinese word for 'tomato juice'?
23. In which city is Bandaranaike International Airport located?
24. In computers, if 'cc' stands for carbon copy, what does 'bcc' stand for?
25. In 1887, what was developed by Adolf Fick to correct irregular astigmatism?
26. The logo of which organization features a burning candle wrapped in barbed wire?
27. Which comic-strip character regards his master as 'that round-headed kid' who brings him his supper dish?
28. Which country has the largest postal network in the world?
29. After how many years is the census carried out in India?

30. What was defined as 'three grains of barley, dry and round, placed end to end lengthwise'?
31. In which organization's garden would you find a statue with an inscription reading 'Let us beat swords into ploughshares'?
32. Which painter painted *Portrait of Doctor Gachet*, *Irises* and *Sunflowers*?
33. Which country has eleven official languages and is called 'the rainbow nation'?
34. In 2000, while addressing the Indian Parliament Bill Clinton said: 'The world is divided between those who have seen the _____ and those who have not.' What was he referring to?
35. The word culinary is derived from a Latin word. What does it mean?
36. How many concentric circles would you see on the emblem of the United Nations?
37. Which spice is called Tamr al-hindi in Arabic?
38. Which function would you be performing if you pressed Ctrl + V?
39. What would you normally use a beanbag for?
40. Which method of producing designs literally means 'painted' in Javanese?
41. Which dry fruit appears as though one of its ends had been forcibly sunk into the end of a pear-shaped swollen stem?
42. How many vowel keys are there at the bottom row of a computer keyboard?
43. In which European capital city is the famous Millennium Dome situated?
44. Which painter used to sign his paintings as Vincent?

45. In USA, the Newberry Medal is awarded for contribution to which form of literature?
46. What are drift, trammel and surrounding different types of?
47. Which is the southernmost national capital in the world?
48. Which fabric are eri, pat and tassar types of?
49. Who is the only president of the USA to have won a Pulitzer Prize?
50. Which mythical animal appears on the flag of Bhutan?

ANSWERS

HISTORY-I

1. The Koh-i-noor diamond
2. Adolf Hitler
3. Mahatma Gandhi
4. Sarvepalli Radhakrishnan
5. New Stone Age
6. He resigned
7. The Manhattan Project
8. Fiddle
9. Shivaji
10. Pilots of Japanese suicide planes
11. Golkonda Fort
12. Mahatma Gandhi
13. Balban
14. Myanmar/Burma
15. Nelson Mandela
16. Sirimavo Bandaranaike
17. Humayun
18. Mandalas
19. Jama Masjid

20. Marathon and Athens
21. Krishnadeva Raya
22. From the River Lena
23. Slavery
24. Marco Polo
25. Chauri-Chaura incident
26. Humayun
27. Chains
28. Sutlej
29. He was hanged with Nathuram Godse for the assassination of Mahatma Gandhi.
30. Rani Laxmibai of Jhansi
31. Mohammed Bin Tughluq
32. Genghis Khan
33. Akbar Shah II
34. Florence Nightingale
35. The Tughluq Dynasty
36. Nelson
37. Bill Clinton
38. Adolf Hitler
39. Salt
40. Oslo
41. Benito Mussolini
42. Nepal
43. Lakshmanasena of the Sena dynasty
44. Shah Jahan
45. Belgium
46. Korean War
47. Winston Churchill
48. The Buddha
49. Harsha

50. Swami Vivekananda

HISTORY-II

1. Mahatma Gandhi
2. Panipat
3. George Yule
4. Taj Mahal
5. Handkerchief
6. The Bastille
7. Tipu Sultan
8. Bahadur Shah II
9. Humayun
10. Pratihara
11. Sadar Diwani Adalat
12. The Bahamani Kingdom
13. Sir Winston Churchill
14. World War I
15. Michelangelo
16. 4 July 1776
17. Victory
18. Samudragupta
19. Attila the Hun
20. Vallabhbhai Patel
21. Alauddin Khilji
22. Shimla
23. Theodore Roosevelt
24. Nana Sahib
25. Mahatma Gandhi
26. Mumtaz Mahal
27. Chandragupta Maurya

28. Koh-i-Noor
29. Rabindranath Tagore
30. Napoleon Bonaparte
31. Khadi
32. C. Rajagopalachari
33. Lala Lajpat Rai
34. Death sentence
35. Elephanta
36. Golden Temple
37. Lotus Temple
38. Copper
39. Rajasthan
40. Winston Churchill
41. Clement Attlee
42. Sarojini Naidu
43. Adolf Hitler
44. Taj Mahal
45. Bindusara
46. The Peacock Throne
47. Netaji Subhas Chandra Bose
48. Sri Lanka
49. Untouchability
50. Science

LANGUAGE AND LITERATURE-I

1. Rudyard Kipling
2. *Uncle Tom's Cabin*
3. *Panchatantra*

4. Gurmukhi
5. *The Guide*
6. *Oliver Twist*
7. *Othello*
8. Paul
9. *Animal Farm*
10. *101 Dalmations*
11. They are all sailors
12. Full stop
13. Subhas Chandra Bose
14. Robinson Crusoe
15. Amrita Pritam
16. Ruskin Bond
17. Shepherdess
18. Rip Van Winkle
19. *Hamlet*
20. *The Adventures of Huckleberry Finn*
21. The Queen of Hearts
22. A ghostwriter
23. Mahashweta Devi
24. Michael Crichton
25. Greek
26. *The Jungle Book*
27. George Eliot
28. *The Taming of the Shrew*
29. Captain Vyom
30. Mahatma Gandhi
31. Hans Christian Anderson
32. Jim Corbett
33. Tears
34. Peter Pan

35. Pali
36. King Arthur
37. Big- Ears
38. *The Treasure Island*
39. Munshi Prechand
40. *Great Expectations*
41. Equine
42. 'Tiger Tiger'
43. Lawyer
44. Sherlock Holmes
45. Buddha
46. Naipaul
47. *Anandamath*
48. A cat
49. *Moby Dick*
50. Leo Tolstoy

LANGUAGE AND LITERATURE-II

1. *Gitanjali*
2. Malgudi
3. *Alice's Adventures in Wonderland*
4. *Godan*
5. Agatha Christie
6. Etcetera
7. The Hogwarts Express
8. Rabindranath Tagore
9. Germany
10. *Pride and Prejudice*
11. Tolkien
12. Banquo

13. George Orwell
14. The Ramayana
15. The Hardy Boys
16. Geppetto
17. Kiran Desai
18. Five Find-outers
19. Hercule Poirot
20. March Hare
21. William Shakespeare
22. Aesop
23. Rudyard Kipling
24. *Sense and Sensibility*
25. *The God of Smalll Things*
26. Don Quixote
27. Graham Greene
28. Kim
29. Spine
30. Louisa May Alcott
31. Flash Gordon
32. Mark Twain
33. *A Suitable Boy*
34. Romeo and Juliet
35. *Les Miserables*
36. Lewis Caroll
37. The Three Musketeers
38. Anne Frank
39. Hogwarts
40. *Jurassic Park*
41. Quasimodo
42. *Uncle Tom's Cabin*
43. Salman Rushdie

44. Jackal
45. Sarojini Naidu
46. *Wuthering Heights*
47. 'If'
48. Antonio
49. Loot
50. 'Night of the Scorpion'

ENTERTAINMENT-I

1. *Sholay*
2. Devika Rani
3. Phantom
4. Shah Rukh Khan
5. Satyajit Ray himself
6. Sunil Dutt
7. Lata Mangeshkar
8. Charlie Chaplin
9. Sanjeev Kumar
10. Moustaches
11. Topi
12. Ustad Alla Rakha
13. Puneet Issar
14. Pavitra Prabhakar
15. Amitabh Bachchan
16. *My Dear Kuttichattan*
17. *Maine Pyar Kiya*
18. Sabu
19. Mithun Chakraborty
20. Michael Jackson
21. Satyajit Ray

22. Paul McCartney
23. Mr Natwarlal
24. *Gandhi*
25. Daniel Craig
26. Vidya Balan
27. Richie Rich
28. *Jeans*
29. Ritwik Ghatak
30. All are gharanas of music
31. *Star Trek*
32. Meercat
33. Mandrake
34. National integration
35. Shaktimaan
36. Jaya Bhaduri
37. Shabana Azmi
38. He-Man
39. Ronald Reagan
40. Macaulay Caulkin
41. Dhanno
42. Bhisham Sahni
43. *Hum Aapke Hain Koun*
44. Amitabh Bachchan
45. Tom Cruise
46. Mr Spock
47. A bicycle
48. Sunil Gavaskar
49. Dilip Kumar
50. *Baghban*

ENTERTAINMENT-II

1. *Aladdin*
2. Meena Kumari
3. Ruskin Bond
4. Anil Kapoor
5. Jadoo
6. *Pather Panchali*
7. Common Man
8. Mahatma Gandhi
9. *Awaara*
10. Amrita Pritam
11. The Great Barrier Reef
12. A.R. Rahman
13. Atal Behari Vajpayee
14. *Black*
15. Rogers
16. Nagesh Kukunoor
17. *The Rising: Ballad of Mangal Pandey*
18. *Dilwale Dulhania Le Jayenge*
19. Aishwarya Rai
20. Riverdale
21. Mahatma Gandhi
22. *The Incredibles*
23. Soorma Bhopali
24. *The Lion King*
25. *Pocahontas*
26. Bugs Bunny
27. Urmila Matondkar
28. Kajol
29. Phantom

30. Walt Disney
31. Amjad Khan
32. *Alam Ara*
33. *Saat Hindustani*
34. Rajesh Khanna
35. Postman
36. Ricky Martin
37. Shabana Azmi
38. Euphoria
39. Shaktimaan
40. *Neecha Nagar*
41. Zakir Hussain
42. Mehmood
43. Jim Carrey
44. *The Lord of the Rings: The Return of the King*
45. R.D. Burman
46. Asha Bhonsle with Code Red
47. Peanuts
48. Akshay Kumar
49. Meg Ryan
50. *Manthan*

GEOGRAPHY-I

1. Kanchenjunga
2. Y
3. Mount Fuji
4. Rio de Janeiro
5. Arizona, Alabama and Alaska
6. Narmada
7. Afghanistan

8. Kilimanjaro
9. Superior
10. Asia
11. Mizoram
12. Volcanic eruptions
13. Lake Baikal
14. China
15. New Guinea
16. Nile
17. Cuttack
18. Niagara Falls
19. Volcanic eruptions
20. Andaman and Nicobar Islands
21. Jharkhand
22. Ho Chi Minh
23. Mount Acconcagua
24. Andhra Pradesh
25. Kanchenjunga
26. Minicoy
27. Mediterranean Sea
28. Yemen
29. Kazakhstan
30. The Zambezi
31. Hanuman
32. Persian Gulf
33. Tamil Nadu
34. Cotopaxi
35. Tokyo
36. India Gate
37. Mount Everest
38. Formosa meaning beautiful

39. Anai Mudi
40. Rock Gardens
41. Rajasthan
42. Pondicherry
43. The Poles
44. Bada Imambara
45. Nalanda
46. Buland Darwaza
47. The Golden Temple of Amritsar
48. Qutb Minar
49. Rashtrapati Bhavan
50. Indonesia

GEOGRAPHY-II

1. Red
2. Chandigarh
3. Arunachal Pradesh
4. Rainbow
5. Sicily
6. Antarctica
7. June
8. The Amazon
9. Hurricane
10. Turkey
11. Qatar
12. Denmark
13. The Andes
14. The Sydney Harbour Bridge
15. Antarctica
16. Pakistan

17. Congo
18. Haflong
19. Vatican City
20. The Niagara Falls
21. Venice
22. The Netherlands
23. Denmark
24. Volga
25. None
26. France
27. New York City
28. Zanzibar and Tanganyika
29. Sutlej
30. Sri Lanka
31. Gobi
32. Karakoram
33. Brahmaputra
34. Paris
35. Singapore
36. Colombia
37. All are beaches in Goa
38. Akbar
39. Hailey's Comet
40. Delta
41. Siachen Glacier
42. Lion
43. Jordan
44. Lightning
45. Taxila
46. Turkey
47. Rajasthan

48. Patna
49. Africa
50. Mount Everest

MYTHOLOGY-I

1. Dussala
2. Shiva
3. Veena
4. His thumb
5. Shatrughna
6. Arjun
7. Menaka
8. Ravana
9. Kaikeyi
10. Surpanakha
11. Kartikeya
12. Rig Veda
13. Parashurama
14. Ass
15. The Ramayana
16. Treta yuga
17. Shanta
18. Kanva
19. Abhimanyu
20. Manu
21. Satyavati
22. Kubera
23. Indra
24. Bhishma
25. Balarama

26. Arjuna
27. He was a cowherd
28. Mareecha
29. Vibhishana
30. Vayu (Pawan)
31. Vaikuntha
32. Dhrishtadyumna
33. Goat
34. Abhimanyu
35. Ambalika
36. Conch shell
37. The bull
38. Durga
39. Dronacharya
40. Meghnad or Indrajit
41. Rama
42. Surya or the Sun god
43. Arjuna
44. Brahma
45. Karna
46. Dasaratha
47. Mathura
48. Hanuman
49. Ashvatthama
50. Valmiki

MYTHOLOGY-II

1. Shiva
2. Yama
3. Draupadi

4. Arjuna
5. Hanuman
6. Karna
7. Mahameru
8. The Gita
9. Apsaras
10. Krishna
11. Sakuni
12. Brahma
13. Jatayu
14. Brahma
15. Fire
16. Krishna
17. Hanuman
18. Veena
19. Gandhari
20. Karna
21. Panchatantra
22. Hiranyakasipu
23. Ninety-nine (99)
24. Dharmadeva
25. Vamana
26. Satrughna
27. Vijaya
28. Jambudvipa
29. Visvamitra
30. The Ramayana
31. Ravana
32. Kansa
33. Ganesha
34. Four

35. Surya or the Sun god
36. Narasimha
37. Rama
38. Brahma
39. Patala
40. Agni
41. Horse
42. Avatara
43. Dussasana
44. Karna
45. Kiskindha
46. Cow
47. Bhima
48. Sarayu
49. Kama
50. Indrajit

SCIENCE-I

1. *Saare Jahan Se Accha*
2. Vertical Take-off and Landing
3. Virus
4. -40 degrees
5. Knee
6. Water
7. Ruby and sapphire
8. Uranus
9. Aspirin
10. The Supermarine Spitfire
11. Lung
12. Logarithms

13. Asterix
14. The bicycle
15. Isaac Newton
16. They are all types of bridges
17. Newton
18. Multiplication
19. The sun
20. The liver
21. Thyroid gland
22. Hydrochloric acid
23. Ringworm. It is a skin infection, the rest are parasites.
24. The teeth
25. An early type of bicycle with one large and one small wheel
26. Cactus
27. Louis Pasteur
28. The eye muscles
29. Titanium
30. First human heart transplant
31. Snoring
32. He was the boy who was given the first vaccination against smallpox by Edward Jenner.
33. Jurassic
34. Mouse
35. You would be mute, unable to speak
36. Leaves
37. Aneroid means 'without liquid'
38. In the old days pipes were made of lead and the word originates from the Latin name of the element, Plumbum.
39. Radium and Polonium

40. Database
41. A boiling kettle
42. Smallpox
43. Hydrogen and oxygen
44. Vinegar
45. Perfect eyesight
46. All are names of computer games
47. Eyes
48. A yard
49. They have walked in space
50. 2

SCIENCE-II

1. The electric battery
2. Earliest type of carbon paper
3. Types of fever
4. Handwriting
5. Kidney and liver
6. Atlas
7. Fingerprints
8. Non-stick
9. Wisdom tooth
10. Dengue
11. Iodine
12. Chikungunya
13. Marie Curie
14. Pain
15. Thailand
16. In the pancreas
17. An equal and opposite reaction

18. Photosynthesis
19. Fungi
20. Lamiaceae
21. Eyes
22. Tungsten, also called Wolfram, has a high melting point
23. Brain
24. Albert Einstein
25. Cools the engine
26. Dogs
27. Oxygen
28. Echo
29. 360 degrees
30. Aluminium
31. Calories
32. 0 and 1
33. Kidneys
34. Tanzania
35. Taking the first letters of all the words in reverse order, we get the word VIBGYOR which is an acronym for the seven colours of the rainbow.
36. Red and green
37. Indivisible
38. Mary had a little lamb
39. Mars
40. Stomach
41. Garbage In Garbage Out
42. C.V. Raman
43. AB group
44. Fahrenheit to Centigrade
45. Ventriloquism
46. A wave

47. Dr Alexander Graham Bell
48. Simple
49. Methane
50. Bhaskara II

INDIA-I

1. Sare Jahan Se Achcha
2. Rath Yatra, Puri
3. Charminar
4. Taj Mahal
5. Trams
6. Chaitra
7. INS Arihant
8. R.K. Laxman
9. An all-women battalion
10. Rakesh Sharma
11. Goa
12. Satyameva Jayate
13. Jaipur
14. Mother Teresa
15. The national flag of India
16. Black Cats
17. National Cadet Corps
18. Ahmedabad
19. IIT Kharagpur
20. The Constitution of India
21. Madan Mohan Malviya
22. Mumbai
23. Agartala
24. Eat it, as it is a type of bread

25. Sun Temple, Konarak
26. Rats
27. Bansuri or flute
28. Sushmita Sen, Miss Universe
29. Pokhran
30. Red Fort
31. Pandit Ravi Shankar
32. Painting
33. Bhima
34. Border Security Force
35. Mahabalipuram
36. Guwahati
37. The Coast Guard
38. Kerala
39. Chipko movement
40. The Palace on Wheels
41. Jaipur
42. Navy Blue
43. Param Vir Chakra
44. New Delhi
45. Currency notes
46. Indian Air Force
47. Koh-i-noor
48. Sari
49. Bihu
50. Damodar Valley Corporation

INDIA-II

1. Bishnoi
2. Kanchenjunga

3. Lotus Temple
4. Bangladesh
5. Clay
6. Papier-maché
7. J.R.D. Tata
8. Goa
9. Tansené
10. M.S. Subbulakshmi
11. Tamil Nadu
12. Mridangam
13. Santoor
14. George Harrison
15. Rajasthan
16. Cinnamon
17. Chicken tikka masala
18. Coconut
19. Parliament House
20. Indelible ink
21. Andhra Pradesh
22. Economy
23. Currency notes
24. Peepal
25. Sri Aurobindo
26. Baba Amte
27. Protima Bedi
28. Meerabai
29. Mohammed Iqbal
30. Lamp/ Lantern
31. Fairy Queen
32. Madhubani
33. Dal

34. Corbett National Park
35. Bismillah Khan
36. The Chhatrapati Shivaji Terminus
37. Jamshedpur
38. Passenger Name Record
39. Warli
40. First film screening
41. Elephant
42. Central Reserve Police Force
43. India
44. Odisha
45. Silvassa
46. Nashik
47. Varanasi
48. National flag of India
49. Mundaka
50. Ten

WILDLIFE-I

1. A colt
2. Birds that lay their eggs in other birds' nests and have the foster parents take care of them e.g. cuckoo
3. None, apes are tail-less
4. Deer
5. Aardvark
6. Goldfish
7. Different subspecies of tiger
8. The elephant
9. Calf
10. The mongoose

11. The Gir forest in Gujarat
12. The Snow Leopard
13. Drones
14. King Cobra
15. Jammu and Kashmir
16. By its teeth
17. Lizard
18. Liger
19. Walrus
20. Lay eggs
21. Cats
22. A brush
23. Nilgai
24. Mad Cow Disease
25. Emu
26. Sloth Bear
27. In its feet
28. Joey
29. Dinosaur
30. Lions
31. Their mother's milk (they are mammals)
32. They cannot fly
33. Beaver
34. Four
35. Australia
36. Elephant
37. Bison
38. Springbok
39. Nectar and pollen
40. Amoeba
41. Basenji

42. Heartbeat
43. Blue Jay
44. Komodo Dragon
45. Elephant
46. Dragonfly
47. Giraffe
48. Polar bears
49. Arabian horse
50. Frog

WILDLIFE-II

1. Dog
2. Vulture
3. Ostrich
4. Scales
5. Musk Deer
6. Giant Panda
7. Adder
8. Ostrich
9. Five
10. Troop
11. Walrus
12. Manipur
13. Black Mamba
14. Cicada
15. Orang National Park
16. Polar bear
17. Kaikadi
18. Indian wild ass
19. Assam

20. Elephant
21. Jaguar
22. Polar bear
23. Arctic fox
24. River Dolphin
25. Elephant
26. Gharial
27. Snail
28. Asian wild ass
29. Turtle
30. Antarctica
31. Woodpecker
32. Tiger
33. Deer
34. Dachshund
35. Earthworm
36. Albatross
37. Lions
38. Hedgehog
39. Cheetah
40. Pebbles
41. Yellow
42. Eagle
43. Monkey
44. Olive Ridley turtles
45. Octopus
46. Tarantula
47. Antelope
48. Meerkat
49. Giant Panda
50. Sundarbans

SPORTS-I

1. 9994
2. Chaturanga
3. Muhammad Ali
4. Rubik's Cube
5. Sunil Gavaskar
6. O.M. Nambiar
7. To sell ice-cream in them
8. Marathon
9. Carrom
10. Boris Becker, 1985
11. Ferenc Puskas
12. Car-racing
13. Two days
14. P.T. Usha
15. Vulture; he was known as The Vulture
16. Sachin Tendulkar
17. Leander Paes
18. US Open
19. East Bengal and Mohun Bagan
20. Dibyendu Barua
21. Barbados
22. 18
23. Football
24. Clive Lloyd
25. Bodyline
26. A bully-off
27. Wrestling
28. Tennis
29. Mansur Ali Khan Pataudi

30. The 1936 Berlin Olympics
31. The host country
32. High jump
33. Muhammad Ali
34. Idi Amin
35. Platform and Springboard
36. Bishen Singh Bedi
37. Jimmy Connors
38. The Azteca Stadium, Mexico City
39. Black and white
40. The Golden Shoe
41. Squash
42. Melbourne Cricket Ground
43. Hesh
44. Golf
45. All England Badminton Championships
46. Thomas Lord
47. Ice Hockey
48. Lifesaving
49. Mexican Wave
50. Bengal

SPORTS-II

1. Greece
2. Black Pearl
3. Two
4. Taekwondo
5. Joshna Chinnappa
6. David Gower
7. Gymnastics

8. Cycling
9. 10,000 m
10. Waqar Younis
11. Madan Lal
12. Australia
13. Volleyball
14. Manchester United
15. Mushtaq Mohammad
16. Cricket
17. Prakash Padukone
18. Table Tennis
19. Mohinder Amarnath
20. Bangkok, in 1966 and 1998
21. Om Agarwal
22. Barcelona
23. Brian Lara
24. West Indies
25. Billiards
26. Kumar Sangakkara
27. Zimbabwe
28. Mary Pierce
29. Sailing
30. Shane Warne
31. Hockey
32. Cafu
33. They do not dip their national flag
34. Swimming
35. Polo
36. Steffi Graf
37. Sachin Tendulkar and Vinod Kambli
38. Allan Border

39. International Master
40. Franz Beckenbauer
41. Croquet
42. Alexander Dityatin
43. 4-3-2-1 formation
44. Clothes-line
45. Cycling
46. Sumo wrestling
47. Arsenal
48. Ashes
49. Sergei Bubka
50. Baseball

MIXED BAG-I

1. Confucius
2. Watch
3. European Union
4. Afghanistan
5. Red
6. Leonardo Da Vinci
7. Doctor
8. Wax
9. Tea
10. Kajal
11. Libra
12. Lock
13. Aung San Suu Kyi
14. Safety razor
15. Easter Island
16. Khaki

17. Doordarshan
18. Leg
19. Applique
20. South Africa
21. Bangladesh
22. 5
23. Machine
24. Phantom
25. Original colonies
26. Red
27. Sun Temple, Konark
28. Umbrella
29. Runway
30. Aquarius
31. Pepper
32. Germany
33. Libya
34. Grand Trunk Road
35. Jawaharlal Nehru
36. Ruby
37. A market
38. They read the same upside down
39. Hippocratic Oath
40. Nepal
41. Antarctica
42. Wheat
43. Bhutan
44. Coffee
45. Curry
46. Pomegranate
47. Rice

48. India
49. Santa Claus
50. Buddhist temple

MIXED BAG-II

1. Clove
2. X
3. Sudoku
4. Cotton
5. Peace
6. White
7. Epsilon
8. Ring
9. Fez
10. Olive
11. Legs
12. At the rate of
13. Water
14. Two
15. Reinhold Messner
16. Boy Scouts
17. Queen Victoria
18. English
19. Lotus
20. Short Messaging Service
21. Zambia
22. Ketchup
23. Colombo
24. Blind carbon copy
25. Contact lens

26. Amnesty International
27. Snoopy
28. India
29. Ten
30. Inch
31. United Nations
32. Vincent Van Gogh
33. South Africa
34. Taj Mahal
35. Kitchen
36. Five
37. Tamarind
38. Pasting
39. Sitting
40. Batik
41. Cashewnut
42. None
43. London
44. Vincent Van Gogh
45. Children's literature
46. Nets
47. Wellington
48. Silk
49. John F. Kennedy
50. Dragon